Washington at Valley Forge

George Washington and the Marquis de Lafayette at Valley Forge, 1777.
From a 1907 painting by John Ward Dunsmore.

Washington at Valley Forge

RUSSELL FREEDMAN

HOLIDAY HOUSE / New York

For Kevin Tidd

The author wishes to thank
Dona M. McDermott,
Archivist of Valley Forge National Historic Park,
for all her help on the map of Valley Forge.

Maps by Heather Saunders

The publisher would like to thank the Fraunces® Tavern Museum
for use of "Washington and Lafayette at Valley Forge 1777–1778"
by John Ward Dunsmore, 1907, which appears on page ii.
Gift of William I. Zabriskie
in memory of the Zabriskie Family, 1966.
2007 Conservation Sponsored by the Color Guard
of the Pennsylvania Sons of the Revolution.
Collection of Fraunces® Tavern Museum.

Every effort was made to attribute the illustrations
to the proper artist. If an artist's name is missing from a caption,
the publisher was unable to confirm that artist.

Library of Congress Cataloging-in-Publication Data
Freedman, Russell.
Washington at Valley Forge / by Russell Freedman. — 1st ed.
p. cm.
ISBN 978-0-8234-2069-8 (hardcover)
1. Washington, George, 1732–1799—Headquarters—
Pennsylvania—Valley Forge—Juvenile literature.
2. Valley Forge (Pa.)—History—18th century—Juvenile literature.
3. Pennsylvania—History—Revolution, 1775–1783—Juvenile literature.
4. United States—History—Revolution, 1775–1783—Juvenile literature.
5. United States. Continental Army—Military life—Juvenile literature.
I. Title.
E234.F74 2008
973.3'341—dc22
2007052467

Contents

Contents

vi

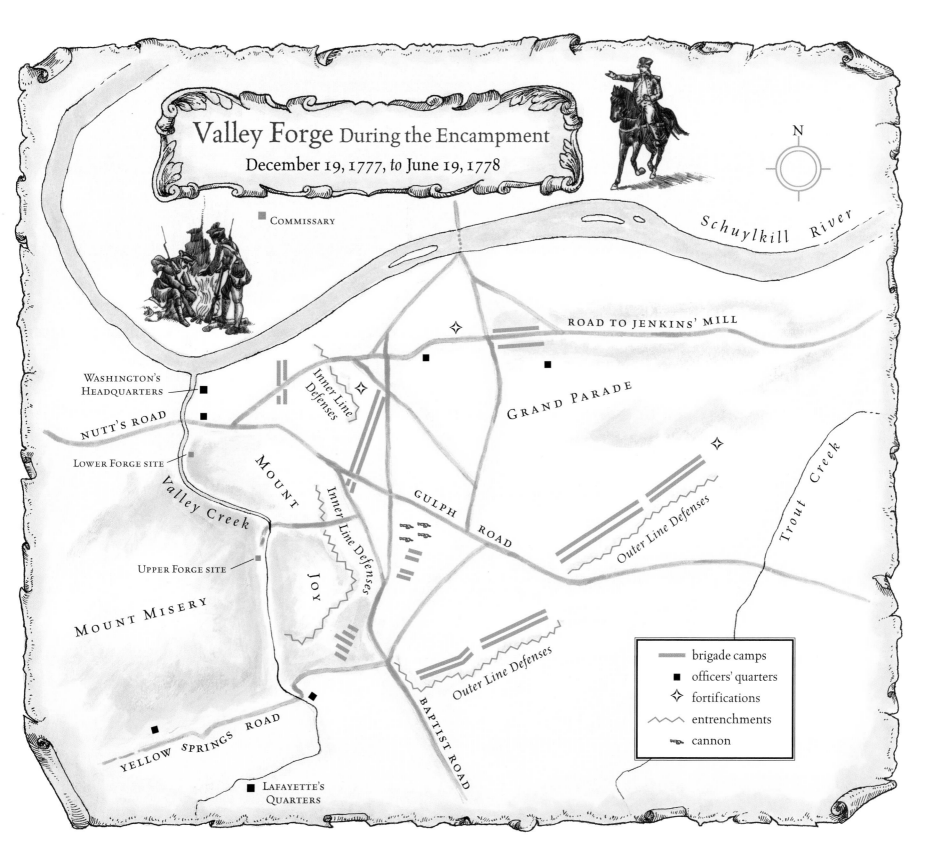

Valley Forge During the Encampment
December 19, 1777, to June 19, 1778

■ COMMISSARY

Schuylkill River

ROAD TO JENKINS' MILL

GRAND PARADE

WASHINGTON'S HEADQUARTERS

NUTT'S ROAD

LOWER FORGE SITE

Inner Line Defenses

MOUNT

Valley Creek

UPPER FORGE SITE

JOY

MOUNT MISERY

Inner Line Defenses

GULPH ROAD

Outer Line Defenses

Trout Creek

Outer Line Defenses

BAPTIST ROAD

YELLOW SPRINGS ROAD

LAFAYETTE'S QUARTERS

N

	brigade camps
■	officers' quarters
✧	fortifications
∿	entrenchments
⌐	cannon

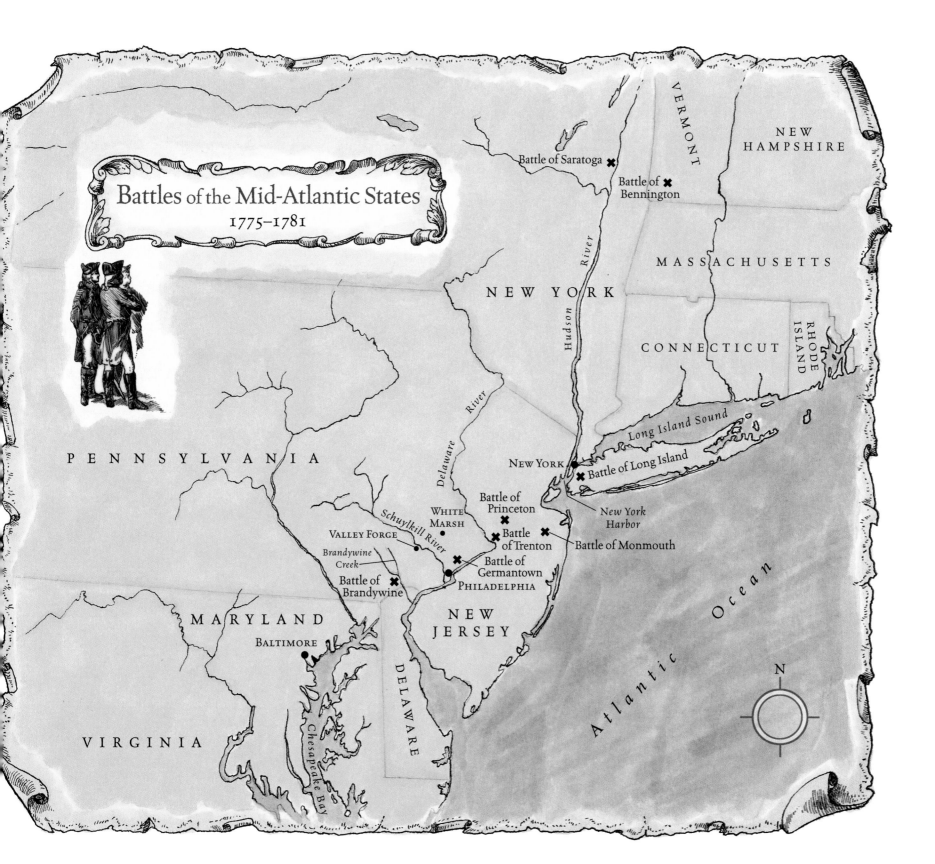

Battles of the Mid-Atlantic States
1775–1781

VERMONT

NEW
HAMPSHIRE

Battle of Saratoga ✖

Battle of
Bennington ✖

MASSACHUSETTS

NEW YORK

CONNECTICUT

RHODE ISLAND

Hudson River

Long Island Sound

New York ● ✖ Battle of Long Island

PENNSYLVANIA

Delaware River

Battle of
Princeton ✖

WHITE
MARSH ●

Schuylkill River

VALLEY FORGE ●

Brandywine
Creek

✖ Battle
of Trenton

New York
Harbor

✖ Battle of Monmouth

Battle of
Germantown

Philadelphia

✖ Battle of
Brandywine

MARYLAND

NEW
JERSEY

BALTIMORE ●

DELAWARE

VIRGINIA

Chesapeake Bay

Atlantic Ocean

N

INTRODUCTION

Against All Odds

GEORGE WASHINGTON'S ARMY almost perished during the winter of 1777 to 1778. It wasn't the coldest winter of the Revolutionary War, or the snowiest. But for Washington's beaten and bedraggled troops camped at Valley Forge, it was the worst of times. Because the army's supply system had collapsed, a lack of food, clothing, and blankets caused terrible hardship and suffering.

That winter, the British had their best chance to crush the American rebellion. Washington himself warned that his army was about to "starve, dissolve, or disperse." And yet the army did not fall apart. In June, the rebels marched out of Valley Forge tested, toughened, and ready to fight.

This is the story of how an embattled band of American revolutionaries struggled against all odds to survive and eventually triumph.

Winter at Valley Forge. *Illustration from an 1898 Scribner's magazine by F. C. (Frederick Coffay) Yohn.*

The march to Valley Forge.
Engraving by Albert Bobbett from an 1877 drawing by Felix O. C. Darley.

ONE

Bloody Footprints in the Snow

PRIVATE JOSEPH PLUMB MARTIN leaned into the icy wind, pushed one sore and aching foot ahead of the other, and kept on marching. With 11,000 other weary soldiers, he was trudging up the Gulph Road, a rutted dirt path that would lead them to a place called the Valley Forge, where the Continental army was to take up winter quarters.

For the past week they had marched through the wintry Pennsylvania countryside in snow, sleet, and freezing rain, toting muskets, knapsacks, and canteens, shivering in the bitter cold, their empty bellies growling and protesting in hunger. They lacked warm clothing and blankets, and they slogged along the road in shoes that were falling apart. When their shoes did give way, the men continued to march on bare, bleeding feet. A division commander reported to General George Washington that half his men were "walking barefooted on the ice or frozen ground."

That's how Private Martin would remember the march years later. "The army was not only starved but naked," he wrote. "The greatest part were not only shirtless and bare-foot, but destitute of all other clothing, especially blankets."

When Martin's own shoes gave out, he found a chunk of raw cowhide and made himself a pair of moccasins "which kept my feet (while they lasted) from the frozen ground, although, as I well remember, the hard edges so galled my ankles, while on a march, that it was with much difficulty and pain that I could wear them afterwards. The only alternative I had was to endure this inconvenience or to go barefoot, as hundreds of my companions had to, till they might be tracked by their blood upon the rough frozen ground. But hunger, nakedness, and sore shins were not the only difficulties we had at that time to encounter. We had hard duty to perform and little or no strength to perform it with."

Martin had just turned seventeen and was already a battle-tested veteran. A husky Connecticut farm boy, he was only fifteen when he went to town with some friends and enlisted in the Continental army in June 1776. The Revolutionary War had broken out the year before, when British troops and Massachusetts minutemen fired on each other at Lexington and Concord.

Young Martin had watched enviously as older boys joined up and marched off to the war. He was eager "to call myself and be called a soldier. . . . I [had] collected pretty correct ideas of the contest between this country [America] and the mother country [Britain]. I thought I was as warm a patriot as the best of them. . . . I felt more anxious than ever to be called a defender of my country." So at fifteen, Martin realized his ambition and became a soldier.

It took General George Washington's suffering army, with its horses, cannons, wagons, baggage, and equipment, a whole week to cover the thirteen miles from their temporary encampment at White Marsh to their winter quarters at the Valley Forge. When they arrived on the evening of December 19, 1777, the place seemed desolate, even haunted—"this wooded wilderness," one officer called it, "the soil thin, uncultivated, and almost uninhabited, without forage and without provisions."

The campsite was a densely wooded plateau about two miles long, bordered by steep hillsides and the swift-flowing Schuylkill River, which served as natural fortifications. Scattered about were a few small houses and some patches of deserted farmland. The whole area had been stripped of food and forage by the British, who had destroyed the old iron forge on Valley Creek that gave the place its name.

Washington had chosen the site because it offered plenty of timber with which to build wooden huts for the winter and because it could be readily defended against an enemy assault. It was also reasonably close—about twenty miles—to Philadelphia, the proud capital of the rebellious American colonies and America's largest city, which had been captured by the British three months earlier. As the American troops at Valley Forge, half-starved, thirsty, and numb with fatigue, pitched their ragged tents and huddled for warmth beside sputtering campfires, the British occupiers of Philadelphia were eating heartily in the city's numerous taverns and sleeping comfortably in billowy feather beds.

Another view by Darley of the troops trudging up the Gulph Road to Valley Forge.

Washington's fellow generals had argued sharply over the selection of winter quarters. It was vital that the army remain close enough to the capital to keep an eye on the enemy and, if opportunity arose, to retake the city from the British. When his officers couldn't agree on a site, Washington chose Valley Forge as the best available compromise. It seemed "a dreary kind of place and uncomfortably provided," the American commander admitted, but he told his soldiers that he himself "would share in the hardship and partake of every inconvenience."

Major General Johann de Kalb, a volunteer from France, was one of the staff officers who disagreed with Washington's choice of a winter campsite. "The idea of wintering in this desert can only have been put into the head of the commanding general by an interested [land] speculator or a disaffected man," he told a friend. "I am satisfied that our present position, if retained, will offer none of the advantages expected of it. On the contrary, the army will be kept in continual alarms from being too near the enemy."

By the time Private Martin's company reached the campsite, it was dark and cold. They had "not a morsel of anything to eat. . . . We were now in a truly forlorn condition—no clothing, no provisions and as disheartened as need be."

Martin was not only hungry; he was "perishing with thirst." He searched for water "till I was weary and came to my tent without finding any." In the darkness, he didn't realize that Valley Creek, which had powered the iron forge destroyed by the British, was just a half mile away. And while there was snow on the ground, it was too thin to scoop up and melt for drinking.

"Fatigue and thirst, joined with hunger, almost made me desperate," Martin recalled. "I felt at that instant as if I would have taken victuals and drink from the best friend I had on earth by force. I am not writing fiction, all are sober realities."

As Martin returned to his tent he spotted two soldiers he didn't know swigging from their canteens. "They told me they had found [water] a good distance off, but could not direct me to the place as it was very dark."

Martin asked for a drink. The soldiers refused, unwilling to share their precious water. But Martin persisted. Finally he persuaded them to sell him a drink "for three pence Pennsylvania currency, which was every cent of property I could then call my own."

General Washington arrived at the campsite the next morning. Rather than move into one of the nearby farmhouses, he pitched his big marquee tent for himself and his aides, as if to show his men that he stood by his word and would share their hardships. Not until most of his troops had some shelter of their own would he move out of the

When they finally reached the campground, the troops huddled around hastily built fires. *Engraving after Darley.*

tent and into a stone house on the encampment grounds. Some of his ranking generals felt no such obligation and immediately took over civilian houses in the vicinity, some as many as three miles from the encampment.

Later that winter, Washington's wife, Martha, joined him at Valley Forge. She was clearly worried about her husband's state of mind. "The General is well, but much worn with fatigue and anxiety," she confided to a friend. "I never knew him to be so anxious as now."

General George Washington, commander in chief of the Continental army, as he appeared in 1780.

Portrait by Charles Willson Peale.

Two

What Is to Become of the Army?

———•———

GENERAL WASHINGTON had plenty of reasons to feel anxious. That autumn the British had captured Philadelphia and defeated the rebels at nearby Brandywine Creek and Germantown. Washington knew that certain high-ranking officers were criticizing him behind his back, questioning his leadership, and suggesting that he should be replaced as commander in chief.

Meanwhile, his troops were short of everything they needed to survive the winter. Much of Washington's time was spent pleading for tents, blankets, and clothing to keep the men from freezing and for rations to keep them from starving.

On December 23, 1777, as his troops were settling into their winter quarters at Valley Forge, Washington wrote to Henry Laurens, president of the Continental Congress, organized by the American colonies as a revolutionary central government. Washington warned of "a dangerous Mutiny" if the army did not receive desperately needed provisions: "I am now convinced, beyond a doubt, that unless some great and capital change suddenly takes place . . . this Army must inevitably be reduced to one or other of these three things. Starve, dissolve, or disperse. . . . Rest assured Sir this is not an exaggerated picture, but that I have abundant reason to support what I say. . . .

"What then is to become of the Army this Winter?"

That winter, the Revolutionary War was well into its third year. The fighting had started at Lexington and Concord on April 19, 1775, when Massachusetts militiamen chased British redcoats back to their base at Boston. Thousands of volunteer militiamen were still blockading Boston a month later when the Second Continental Congress met in Philadelphia on May 10, 1775.

Delegates from all thirteen colonies—they did not yet call themselves states—attended the Congress. (Georgia did not send delegates to the Congress till July.) Despite the battles at Concord and Lexington, some delegates still hoped for a peaceful resolution of the colonies' dispute with England. They were not yet willing to break away from the Mother Country. Other delegates insisted on independence. They wanted to throw off the yoke of British rule and govern themselves. They were willing to fight for the freedom to develop their own society in the way that they wished.

George Washington, a delegate from Virginia, was for independence. He arrived in Philadelphia on horseback, wearing his splendid buff-and-blue militia uniform—a sign that he was ready, if necessary, to join the fight. A wealthy plantation owner and a colonel in the Virginia militia, he had won a hero's reputation years earlier during the French and Indian War. Washington stood "straight as an Indian," said a friend. He had the commanding appearance of a military leader.

"He has so much martial dignity in his deportment that you would distinguish him to be a general and a soldier from among a thousand people," wrote Benjamin Rush, a Philadelphia physician, Congressional delegate, and staunch revolutionary. "There is not a king in Europe who would not look like a *valet de chambre* [a man's male servant] by his side."

Washington's height has been estimated from measurements sent to his tailor in London and those taken after death for his mahogany coffin. They suggested that he was just over six feet three inches tall—at least a head taller than the average male at that time. When he entered a room, everyone had to look up to him. Now in his mid-forties, he was still trim and muscular, with broad shoulders, long arms and legs, and unusually large hands and feet. "He had the largest pair of hands I ever saw," wrote his friend the Marquis de Lafayette, and he could "hurl a stone a prodigious distance."

Washington carried faint pockmarks on his nose, a reminder of a youthful bout with smallpox. A big-boned giant of a man, he could appear awkward while seated. But once in motion, he carried himself with the flowing coordination of an athlete. He was an enthusiastic dancer and a superb horseman. Thomas Jefferson called him "the best horseman of his age, and the most graceful figure that could be seen on horseback."

Washington was the only delegate to attend meetings of the Continental Congress in uniform. He was asked to chair four committees concerned with military readiness. And when the delegates voted to "adopt" the militiamen blockading Boston as a new "American Continental Army," Washington was the unanimous choice to lead the army as its commander in chief. Until then, there had been no such thing as an "American Army," only individual state militias. As a southerner and Virginia's most famous war hero, in command of thousands of New England troops, Washington could help unite the colonies "better than any other person in the Union," said Massachusetts delegate John Adams.

While Washington had come to Philadelphia dressed for war, he seemed taken aback by his selection as commander in chief. True enough, he had fought bravely in the French and Indian War, but that was two decades earlier. He had never commanded a unit larger than a regiment, he knew little about deploying artillery or maneuvering cavalry, and he had no experience planning grand strategies or military tactics. He would be in command of a makeshift army of volunteers with sketchy training and scarcely enough gunpowder to keep their muskets firing. And they would be facing disciplined, battle-tested British regulars belonging to the most powerful army on earth.

"I beg it may be remembered by every Gentleman in the room," Washington warned his fellow Congressional delegates, "that I this day declare with the utmost sincerity, I do not think myself equal to the Command I am honored with."

And in a letter to his wife, Martha, he insisted, "so far from seeking this appointment, I have used every endeavor in my power to avoid it, not only from my unwillingness to part from you and the family, but from a consciousness of its being a trust too great for my capacity."

Compared to the seasoned British officers he would be facing on the battlefield, Washington worried that he was a rank military amateur. Before leaving Philadelphia to take up his new post, he bought several books on military tactics and strategy. He was determined to teach himself how to organize an army and become a general.

Washington took command of 16,000 volunteer militiamen outside British-occupied Boston on July 3, 1775. The Continental Congress had not yet declared independence. Even so, Congress had announced that the colonists would fight to preserve their liberties rather than submit to tyranny. In response, King George III of England had ordered that the American rebels be put down by force.

Washington takes command of the Continental army at Cambridge, Massachusetts, July 3, 1775.
Illustration by Charles Stanley Steinhart from Harper's Weekly, July 10, 1875.

Some historians say this ceremony could not have taken place as pictured here; they argue that the Continental army was not yet well enough trained to march in a formal review.

Washington now was in charge of those rebels besieging Boston, keeping some 10,000 British troops bottled up inside the city. For more than eight months, he directed the siege from his headquarters across the Charles River in Cambridge, where he pored over maps, studied intelligence reports, and searched for weak points in the British defenses.

Early in March 1776, Washington's army took possession of Dorchester Heights, putting the city of Boston and most of the harbor within range of American cannons. Rather than risk senseless slaughter, British General William Howe sent out a flag of truce and offered to evacuate the city peacefully. On March 17, the British forces sailed away, surrendering Boston to General Washington and his joyous troops.

Hoping now for a quick American victory, Washington marched his ragtag army south to confront the British in the New York area. On July 9, 1776, he ordered that the text of the Declaration of Independence—approved by Congress five days earlier—be read aloud to the assembled troops at New York. "The General hopes that this important event will serve as a fresh incentive to every officer and soldier to act with fidelity and courage," Washington announced. The troops roared their approval. Dismissed, they made their way to the fifteen-foot-high gilded statue of King George III on horseback that stood on iron-fenced Bowling Green, and with a jubilant crowd of civilians pulled the royal statue from its base and down to the ground. Later, it was melted down and the metal molded into 42,000 bullets for the Continental army's guns.

By then, the British had landed 32,000 fully equipped men in the vicinity of New York. It was the largest expeditionary force Great Britain had ever sent overseas. Along with the redcoats, the British regulars, the force included a large contingent of Hessians, German mercenaries paid by George III to fight for England.

Washington had been able to muster about 17,000 men in New York. Unlike the professional soldiers serving England, Washington's troops were either poorly trained state militia or newly recruited Continentals, as his regulars were called. What followed was a swift succession of defeats. In battle after battle, the Americans were driven out of New

The Battle of Long Island, August 27, 1776. This painting by Alonzo Chappel shows American troops retreating across Gowanus Creek in the face of a heavy British attack. The Americans suffered a terrible defeat that day, with more than a thousand casualties.

York, withdrawing from Long Island in August, from New York Island (Manhattan) in September, and finally fleeing across the Hudson River to New Jersey, then retreating westward to the Delaware River and Pennsylvania.

"I made my escape as fast as I could," recalled Michael Graham, an eighteen-year-old militiaman at the time, following a battle on Long Island. "It is impossible for me to describe the confusion and horror of the scene, the artillery flying with chains over the horses' backs, our men running in almost every direction, and run which way they would, they were almost sure to meet the British or Hessians." Graham got away by jumping into "a swamp or marsh through which a great many of our men were retreating. Some of them were mired and calling out to their fellows for God's sake to help them out; but every man was intent on his own safety. . . . Of the eight men that were taken from the company to which I belonged the day before the battle, I only escaped. The others were either killed or taken prisoner."

On December 11, what was left of the Continental army—not much more than 5,000 troops, one-third of them too sick or hungry to serve—barely escaped capture by crossing the Delaware into Pennsylvania. Unless a new army could be raised, and quickly, Washington warned, "I think the game will be pretty well up."

The struggle for American independence appeared to be a lost cause. With New York and New Jersey in British hands, Congress fled from Philadelphia to Baltimore on December 12. Some delegates were ready to give up and sue for peace. Washington's shrinking army seemed doomed. What was needed, he realized, was to "strike some Stroke," to carry out a bold move, a surprise attack that would revive the rebels' sagging morale.

Now, for the first time, the Continental army went on the offensive. On December 25, 1776, in the dead of night, Washington personally led 2,400 men across the ice-choked Delaware River in a driving sleet storm and stormed the Hessian garrison at Trenton, taking more than 900 prisoners. "Come there about daybreak [December 26] and beat the dam [sic] Hessians," Sergeant Samuel McCarthy of Virginia recorded in his journal.

A week later, Washington led another surprise attack, seizing the British garrison at Princeton. An eyewitness reported that the redcoats retreated "in a most infernal sweat, running, puffing, and blowing and swearing at being so outwitted." These two surprise victories cleared most of western New Jersey of enemy troops, allowed Congress to return to Philadelphia, and sent American morale soaring.

In January 1777, Washington moved his troops to winter quarters in the rugged hill country around Morristown, New Jersey. There he began the task of rebuilding his depleted forces. When he took command of the Continental army, it was made up

Washington at Valley Forge

This depiction of Washington crossing the ice-choked Delaware River on Christmas night, 1776, painted around 1912 by Henry Mosler, captures the heroic spirit of that venture but gets some important details wrong. The boats used for the crossing were actually high-walled barges, similar to the landing craft used for amphibious assaults in World War II. Everyone stood up in them.
If Washington had been standing in a boat of this size, he would have been hurled headlong into the ice.

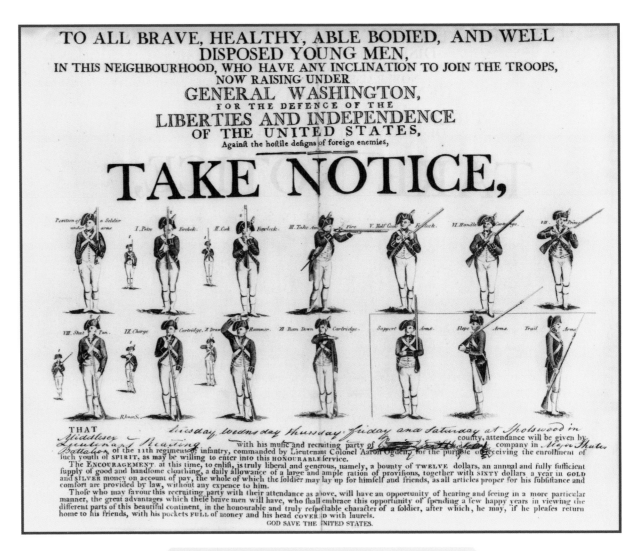

This Continental army recruiting poster from 1775 offered new recruits "a bounty of twelve dollars."

mostly of volunteer militia, part-time citizen soldiers who were neither well trained nor well equipped. Many of them were farmers who insisted on returning to their fields at harvesttime. Washington was convinced that the war could never be won with such short-term volunteers, no matter how dedicated they might be to the cause of liberty. To fight the British, he needed a professional army of disciplined troops who had signed on for the duration. "To expect then the same service from Raw, and undisciplined Recruits as from Veteran soldiers," he explained, "is to expect what never did, and perhaps never will happen."

Congress had authorized an army of 20,000 troops, but as the war continued, Washington had trouble persuading his experienced veterans to stay on when their enlistments were up. By the beginning of 1777, his army was far below authorized strength. At one point, as enlistments expired, Washington may have had as few as 3,000 able-bodied troops under his command to face a British army ten times as large. He ordered each of his commanders to conceal the real number and to "give out your strength to be twice what it is." If the British realized how weak the American army really was, they would strike a blow that could quickly end the war.

Encamped at Morristown, Washington spent much of the winter waiting for new recruits to show up. Meanwhile, recognizing his limited resources, he had to face what he called "the melancholy Truths." His surprise attacks on small British outposts at Trenton and Princeton had raised rebel spirits but had not inflicted serious military damage on the enemy. The war so far had shown that the rebels could not compete on equal terms with the British on a conventional battlefield. Washington's troops had been beaten again and again; they had never defeated the main British army.

Consulting with his senior officers, Washington turned to a revised strategy. His chief responsibility was to ensure the survival of the Continental army. The only way to win the war, he decided, was to outlast the British, to wear them down until they wearied of the conflict.

If the Continental army held out long enough, Washington believed, the British would tire of the war and would recognize American independence. From then on he would fight a defensive war, avoiding pitched battles unless the odds were greatly in his favor, shrugging off defeats as long as he kept his army together. His goal for now was not to occupy new ground but to "harass their troops to death" while preserving his army, to employ hit-and-run surprise raids that had worked so well at Trenton and Princeton.

By the summer of 1777, Washington again had a sizable army. Some 9,000 new regulars, or Continentals, had enlisted—this time for three years or the duration of the war. But even with increased manpower, the inexperienced Americans were no match for seasoned British professionals. In September, at Brandywine Creek in Pennsylvania, rebel troops attempting to defend Philadelphia were routed by the British, who marched into the American capital two weeks later. Members of Congress fled the city again, this time taking up temporary quarters in the country town of York, Pennsylvania.

In October Washington's army, attempting to surprise the British at Germantown, Pennsylvania, suffered another bloody defeat. At a crucial point in the battle, American

The ill-fated Battle of Germantown, October 4, 1777. Confused by heavy fog and smoke, the Americans fired on one another.
Engraving by George Illman from a drawing by Christian Schuessele.

troops fired on one another amid dense fog and smoke, allowing the British to regroup and forcing the Americans to retreat. "The foggy still morning . . . and the body of smoke from the firing absolutely prevented our seeing the enemy till they had advanced close upon us," Colonel Timothy Pickering of Massachusetts recorded in his journal. "The fog blinded the enemy as well as ourselves, though it certainly injured us most."

Up north, meanwhile, the rebels' fortunes turned out to be very different. Americans commanded by General Horatio Gates were battling a British force led by General John Burgoyne, who had marched down from Canada intending to seize the Hudson River Valley and cut off New England from the rest of the colonies. Thousands of New England militiamen had rallied to reinforce Gates's Continental regulars. The British found themselves outnumbered for once, cut off from their supply lines, and marooned in the northern wilderness. On October 17, following the Battle of Saratoga, Burgoyne was forced to surrender with 6,000 survivors of his battered army, handing the greatest American victory of the war to General Gates.

The triumph at Saratoga raised questions about Washington's leadership among members of Congress and some of his own officers. They contrasted Gates's success with Washington's failure to prevent the British capture of Philadelphia. How could Washington have lost so many battles? His enemies began to whisper behind his back about replacing him with Horatio Gates as the army's commander in chief.

By now, another winter was approaching. Washington needed a winter camp where he could rest and reorganize his bedraggled Continentals, a place close enough to Philadelphia to maintain pressure on the British, yet far enough away to guard against surprise attacks. The place he chose was Valley Forge.

General Horatio Gates, hero of Saratoga. Some congressmen and army officers thought that Gates should replace Washington as commander in chief of the Continental army.

Standing ankle-deep in a snowdrift, Washington and Lafayette visit the troops.
Engraving by Henry Bryan Hall, 1857, from a painting by Alonzo Chappel.

THREE

"We Were Determined to Persevere"

———•———

ON THAT FIRST BITTERLY COLD NIGHT at Valley Forge, the wind whipped through the leafless forest as Washington's footsore soldiers pitched camp on the frozen ground. Men shivered in drafty tents. Those without blankets to cover themselves huddled miserably around hastily built fires.

The army now numbered about 11,000 men. A quarter of them, at least, were too ill and poorly clothed to perform their duties. At times, according to James Thacher, a young surgeon's mate from Massachusetts, there were not enough able-bodied men "to discharge the basic duties of the camp."

"Why are we sent here to starve and freeze?" Dr. Albigence Waldo, an army physician with the First Connecticut Infantry, complained to his diary. "There comes a soldier; his bare feet are seen thro' his worn out shoes, his legs nearly naked from the tattered remains of an only pair of stockings, his breeches not sufficient to cover his nakedness, his shirt hanging in strings, his hair dishevelled, his face meager; his whole appearance pictures a person forsaken and discouraged."

Carrying firewood. The troops soon moved from canvas tents to small log huts heated by fireplaces.

Washington ordered the construction of log huts "that will be warm and dry," to house the men before everyone began to freeze to death. The structures were to be fourteen feet wide, sixteen feet long, and six-and-a-half feet high, each with a fireplace at the rear. Twelve men would be assigned to each hut. Officers' huts would be less crowded with fewer occupants. Until the huts were built, the men would have to make do in their tents.

"Our prospect was indeed dreary," Private Joseph Plumb Martin recalled. "In our miserable condition, to go into the wild woods and build us habitations to *stay* (not to *live*) in, in such a weak, starved and naked condition, was appalling in the highest degree, especially to New Englanders, unaccustomed to such kind of hardships at home.

"However, there was no remedy, no alternative but this or dispersion. But dispersion, I believe, was not thought of, at least, I did not think of it. We had engaged in the defense of our injured country and we were determined to persevere as long as such hardships were not altogether intolerable."

During the army's first two days at Valley Forge, food rations were so scarce, all Martin could find to eat was "half of a small pumpkin, which I cooked by placing it upon a rock, the skin side uppermost, and making a fire upon it. By the time it was heated through I devoured it with as keen an appetite as I should a pie made of it at some other time."

Martin's flame-singed pumpkin was at least a break from the men's usual fare. They often had "firecake" (tasteless patties made of flour and water, baked on hot stones) for breakfast, for dinner, and for supper, sometimes along with "pepper hot soup" (a thin tripe broth flavored by a handful of peppercorns).

One day just before Christmas, food rations ran out completely. Chants of "No meat! No meat!" spread through the camp. Some of the men began to imitate screeching owls and cawing crows, suggesting that they might fly their coops like birds of prey and march into the countryside to find food at the point of their bayonets. Officers raced back and forth among the tents, their swords drawn, shouting for the men to quiet down. Brigadier General James Varnum of Rhode Island warned Washington: "The men must be supplied or they cannot be commanded."

Clothing was as scarce as food. Washington reported that "no less than 2,898 Men now in Camp [are] unfit for duty because they are bare foot and otherwise naked." Two other necessities—soap and candles—were also in short supply. Without candles, the men could not read or write after dark. Without soap, they had a hard time bathing and, as a result, were often infected with lice.

The army was short of almost everything needed to sustain life, "destitute of every comfort," as Brigadier General George Weedon of Virginia put it. The officials responsible for supplying the troops—the quartermaster general and the commissary general—were appointed by Congress. For months, Washington had been pleading with Congress for more supplies. He wanted to know why the basic needs of his army were not being met.

"Since the Month of July," Washington reported, "we have had no assistance from the Quartermaster Genl." He warned, "I do not know from what cause this alarming deficiency or rather total failure of supplies arises, but unless more vigorous exertions and better regulations take place . . . immediately, the army must dissolve."

As the Americans built their winter huts, the British were ringing Philadelphia with defensive fortifications. Some members of Congress complained that by going into winter quarters, Washington had left the surrounding countryside unprotected. Washington was furious. In a blistering reply, he heaped scorn on the armchair soldiers in Congress, who had no experience in military matters, and he defended the performance of his army:

"I can assure those Gentlemen that it is a much easier and less distressing thing to draw remonstrances in a comfortable room by a good fire side than to occupy a cold bleak hill and sleep under frost and Snow without Cloaths or Blankets; however, although they seem to have little feeling for the naked, and distressed Soldier, I feel superabundantly for them,

Building huts. Eventually
more than a thousand
log huts were constructed,
creating a small city.
Drawing by Darley.

and from my Soul pity those miseries, wch. [which], it is neither in my power to relieve or prevent."

Washington ended his letter by reminding Congress that "upon the ground of safety and policy, I am obliged to conceal the true State of The Army from public view."

Washington's aides had seen him lose his temper before, usually when supplies failed to arrive. While he was generally calm and self-controlled, his "temper was naturally irritable," a friend observed, and when "it broke its bonds, he was most tremendous in his wrath." But his aides also witnessed another side of Washington's character. Enlisted men would come to the general's headquarters and inform him respectfully that they had seen no meat for days, that their rations weren't enough to keep hunger at bay. Those who saw Washington speak with these men reported that at times his eyes filled with tears.

On Christmas Day, snow was falling. The commissary department reported that there were only twenty-five barrels of flour left. "We have hardly been here six days, and are already suffering from want of everything," General de Kalb wrote. "The men have had neither meat nor bread for four days, and our horses are often left for days without any fodder. What will be done when the roads grow worse, and the season more severe?"

"We are still in tents when we ought to be in huts," Dr. Waldo complained. "The poor sick suffer much in tents this cold weather."

As if conditions weren't bad enough, the army's starving horses began to drop dead. Each horse needed twelve pounds of hay and eight pounds of grain a day, and when this forage ran out, one by one horses toppled silently to the ground. Before the winter ended, some seven hundred horses would perish, and the stench of their decaying bodies hung heavily over the camp. Without horses, soldiers yoked themselves to wagons for hauling wood and provisions or carried heavy loads on their backs.

As Washington struggled to hold his army together, he was keenly aware of a rising tide of impatience with his leadership and of the criticism being voiced in Congress and by a few army officers. Friends had warned him that "Secret enemies" were trying to "Rob you of the great and truly deserved esteem your country has for you . . . [and] lessen you in the minds of the people." A small group of officers led by Brigadier General Thomas Conway was maneuvering behind the scenes to damage Washington's reputation and undermine his control over the army. They wanted to remove Washington as commander in chief and replace him with General Horatio Gates, who had defeated the British at Saratoga.

Their strategy, Washington was told, was making people "believe that you have had three or four times the number [of troops] of the Enemy, and have done nothing, that Philadelphia was given up by your Mismanagement and that you have missed many opportunities of defeating the enemy."

Historians call this scheme the Conway Cabal, but it is not clear if it was actually a secret plot to replace Washington or simply a lot of loose talk by some disgruntled and envious generals. Washington knew that he still had the confidence of most of his officers and the devotion of his troops. He held his temper in check and coolly took the offensive. He demanded that a congressional investigating committee visit Valley Forge to see firsthand the army's true condition.

Darley's drawing of the army in camp.

Washington knew that his critics expected the army to perform feats that only a much stronger force could accomplish. Yet he had to conceal the alarming weakness of his forces from the British. "My enemies take an ungenerous advantage of me," he told Henry Laurens, president of Congress. "They know the delicacy of my situation and that motives of policy deprive me of the defense I might otherwise

Washington inspects the troops. *From a 1911 painting by Edward P. Moran.*

make against the insidious attacks. They know I cannot combat their insinuations, however injurious, without disclosing secrets it is of the utmost moment to conceal."

The secret that he dare not reveal—the appalling condition of the Continental army—was one of the few weapons he had left. "Next to being strong," he wrote, "it is best to be thought so by the enemy."

FOUR

"A Cavalcade of Wild Beasts"

THE YEAR 1778 started off with a bang. On January 5, several people in British-occupied Philadelphia spotted a large barrel, or keg, floating in the Delaware River. Two boys rowed out to see what the keg contained. It exploded on contact, alarming sentries on the waterfront and on British warships anchored nearby.

When other floating kegs appeared, a rumor spread that they were occupied by armed rebels attempting to sneak into Philadelphia and take the city by surprise. The British opened fire, bombarding the kegs from warships and from cannons along the shore. "Whole broadsides were poured into the Delaware," one newspaper reported. "In short, not a wandering chip, stick, or drift log but felt the vigor of British arms."

As it turned out, the floating kegs were the brainchild of David Bushnell, the American explosives expert. Earlier, in New York, he had invented underwater mines, set off by a timing device, to be planted by his one-man submarine, the American Turtle. In place of a timing device, the Philadelphia kegs, packed with gunpowder, had a contact mechanism that triggered the explosion.

The night before, Bushnell had set the kegs adrift upriver from Philadelphia. They

The Battle of the Kegs,
January 5, 1778.

were supposed to drift with the tide among British warships and transports and explode when they bumped into a ship. But the Delaware's shifting currents swept the kegs off course, and they were spotted before they could accomplish their mission.

The daylong British artillery barrage gave the rebels a chance to mock "the bravery, and military skill of the royal navy" in its victorious battle "against the enemy, the kegs." Francis Hopkinson, a signer of the Declaration of Independence, wrote a fifteen-stanza satirical poem, "The Battle of the Kegs," poking fun at the British, which was printed in rebel newspapers from Boston to Savannah. The poem soon became a wildly popular ditty, sung with gusto in America's taverns and, perhaps, by the shivering hut builders at Valley Forge.

The last stanza went like this:

Such feats did they perform that day
Against those wicked kegs, sir
That years to come, if they get home
They'll make their boasts and brags, sir.

Work on the log huts was moving ahead more slowly than planned. Construction was held up by a shortage of nails, axes, and other tools, by the men's exhaustion, and by spells of nasty weather. A heavy snowfall one day was followed by rain the next, and hut builders hauling logs had to slog through slush and mud. Washington offered a prize of twelve dollars to the twelve-man team that finished a hut in "the quickest and most workmanlike manner."

Washington's Valley Forge headquarters house as it looks today. He lived and worked here, along with Martha and a number of aides.

While the huts were going up, Washington moved from his big marquee tent to a five-room stone house at the edge of the encampment, which he rented from the owner, Isaac Potts. The house became his command headquarters. He took over one of the downstairs rooms as his office, where he kept his valuable papers in a secret box built into the wall below a window. The other downstairs room became a combination sitting room and office for Washington's staff. Upstairs were three small bedrooms. Washington, and later Martha, slept in one, while the other two bedrooms were occupied by some of the general's aides.

Snowstorms continued to batter the encampment. "For

Washington's personal desk. His office occupied one of the house's five rooms.

A reconstructed hospital hut at Valley Forge.

a week past we have had snow, and as cold weather as I almost ever knew at home," Lieutenant Colonel John Brooks of Massachusetts wrote to a friend on January 5. "To see our poor brave fellows living in tents, bare-footed, bare-legged, bare-breeched, etc. etc., in snow, in rain, in marches, in camp, and on duty, without being able to supply their wants is really distressing. Where the fault is I know not. . . . Under all those disadvantages no men ever shew more spirit or prudence than ours. In my opinion nothing but virtue has kept our army together through this campaign."

As many as one man in four was unfit for duty. The encampment was ravaged by "camp fever" (typhus, spread by fleas, lice, and mites); by "putrid fever" (typhoid, transmitted by contaminated food and water); and by dysentery, smallpox, and other highly infectious diseases. Hundreds of ailing soldiers were sent to the camp hospital that had been set up in an old schoolhouse. Others were transported in carts or wagons over bumpy roads to faraway hospitals in Pennsylvania and New Jersey.

Inside the hospital hut—the examination table.

"Three more of my Regt died last night and this day were deacently [sic] buried," Colonel Israel Angell of Rhode Island recorded in his diary. "It is a very alarming time amongst us [as] the troops are very sickly and die fast." By winter's end, as many as 2,500 soldiers at Valley Forge would die from exposure, malnutrition, or disease.

Despite severe hardships, the camp hummed with activity. The winds that howled through the trees carried the sounds of hammers, axes, saws, and shovels at work. Log huts appeared on the landscape, lookout towers and fortifications were constructed and strengthened, and hundreds of men performed guard duty every day. To overcome the shortage of warm clothing, all the occupants of a hut or tent would contribute to a complete outfit for whoever was called to duty out in the cold.

Paper money issued by the Continental Congress. Some farmers and merchants refused to take the bills, considering them worthless. They demanded "real money"—gold or silver coins.

Foraging parties in search of provisions moved constantly in and out of camp. Some farmers in the area refused to sell food or livestock in exchange for the almost worthless paper money printed by the Continental Congress. Other farmers took their goods into Philadelphia to sell to the British, who paid high prices in gold. When foraging soldiers found goods or cattle stashed away in barns or hidden in nearby woods, they were authorized to seize them as the spoils of war.

Private Joseph Plumb Martin was assigned to foraging duty. He joined a detachment consisting "of a lieutenant, a sergeant, a corporal, and eighteen privates." Their orders were "to go into the country on a foraging expedition, which was nothing more nor less than to procure provisions from the inhabitants . . . at the point of a bayonet."

Like Martin himself, a large number of the soldiers at Valley Forge were teenagers. Almost all the enlisted men were between fifteen and twenty-five years of age, with some drummer boys as young as twelve. Many were recent immigrants to America, mostly from Ireland, Scotland, England, and Germany, but also from a dozen other European nations. Among them were Protestants of various denominations, Roman Catholics, and Jews. While the enlisted men came from many walks of life, most were unmarried, landless, and poor. The army offered them a steady wage, the promise of land bounties and monetary bonuses, a chance to test their courage and skills, and the pride of taking part in the cause of liberty. They believed that a free and independent America would offer men like themselves opportunities and a brighter future.

African Americans served alongside whites in almost every regiment—the last racially integrated American army units until the Korean War of the 1950s. Almost 10 percent of the troops at Valley Forge were either free blacks who had volunteered or slaves serving in place of their owners (who wanted to avoid being drafted) in exchange for the promise of freedom if they survived the war. In one Virginia brigade, 13 percent of the troops were black. Some slaves changed their names to express their goal: Dick Freedom, Jeffrey Liberty, Jupiter Free among them. Blacks were accepted by their fellow troops as "brother soldiers," the term used by enlisted men when they spoke to or about each other.

One of the first soldiers to die at Valley Forge was an African American known to history only as Jethro. On Christmas Day, 1777, surgeon's mate Jonathan Todd of Connecticut wrote to his father: "Jethro, a Negro from Guilford . . . died in his tent, the first man that hath died in camp belonging to our regt."

Most American Indians, hoping to preserve their culture and protect their lands from American settlers, sided with the British. But some tribes supported the Americans. Several hundred Indians enlisted in the Continental army, while many others served in specialized units as scouts.

Along with the troops, about 450 women and 300 children were officially attached to the army at Valley Forge. A few were the wives of officers on extended visits, but most of the women were the wives and girlfriends of enlisted men who followed the troops year round and lived near them in camp. Called "camp followers," they cooked, sewed, mended, and

An American soldier at Valley Forge, as depicted in an 1860 illustration from *Harper's* magazine. He wears a patched and tattered uniform and has leggings but no boots. His bare toes grip the snow.

Camp followers: women and children, often families of enlisted men, accompanied most eighteenth-century armies. This drawing depicts Hessian troops on the march, with camp followers tagging along.

Washington at Valley Forge

laundered, nursed the sick and wounded, and at times, took over a gun when their husbands fell. The army recognized their importance to the men and provided rations and supplies for soldiers' families.

Altogether, the foot soldiers of the Continental army were a tough and independent crowd, men who did not bend easily to the spit and polish of strict military discipline. They defied regulations about hair length. They decorated their uniforms, such as they were, with ribbons, feathers, and fur. Since each state issued its own style and color of uniform, there was no consistency. Many men wore fringed hunting shirts and leather leggings they had brought from home. Without hot running water or showers, and with a shortage of soap, they had little chance or inclination to bathe or wash the tattered clothing they had worn for months. One soldier described these enlisted men on the march as "a cavalcade of wild beasts."

"The greatest part of them have not before seen Service," the Massachusetts Provincial Congress informed Washington. "And altho' naturally brave and of good understanding, yet for want of Experience in military Life, have but little knowledge of divers things most essential to the preservation of Health and even of Life. The Youth in the Army are not possess'd of the absolute Necessity of Cleanliness in their Dress, and Lodging, continual Exercise, and strict Temperance, to preserve them from Diseases frequently prevailing in Camps."

Washington had warned Congress that without adequate supplies, "this army must . . . dissolve." He worried about the troops' morale. And he lived in fear of a possible mutiny. At times there were no funds to pay the enlisted men. When they did receive their pay, it didn't go far. A small bread pie sold by the peddlers who visited the camp cost two dollars. A private's pay was eight dollars a month.

Now and then, men would begin chanting in their hut: "No pay! No clothes! No provisions! No rum!" The rebellious chant would be taken up by other huts throughout the camp. Scores of enlisted men simply gave up and deserted, evading the camp's sentries

Washington and Lafayette visit the cold and hungry troops in this 1843 painting by A. Gibert.

at night and hiding in the woods until the coast was clear. When they were caught, they were flogged. Fifty lashes was the standard punishment. Repeat offenders were hanged.

Washington had asked Congress to send a delegation to Valley Forge, where the politicians who had criticized his leadership could see for themselves the desperate conditions at the army's winter camp. A committee of five congressmen finally arrived on January 24. Washington greeted them ceremoniously and made sure that they were comfortably settled in a large stone house about three miles from the encampment. It would be up to these skeptical, questioning congressmen to assess the army's situation firsthand. Like the British, they had been led to believe that the army was much larger and stronger than it actually was.

They were shocked by what they found. On February 2, 1778, Gouverneur Morris, a congressman from New York, wrote to a friend that the committee had witnessed "the skeleton of an army . . . in a naked, starving condition, out of health, out of spirits."

FIVE

"Congress Does Not Trust Me"

❖

BY THE BEGINNING OF FEBRUARY, almost all the troops had moved from tents to dirt-floored wooden huts they had constructed themselves. Army engineers had marked the sites where each brigade should build, and when finished, the huts stood side by side in orderly rows, each doorway facing a brigade "street." More than 2,000 of these log huts had been built. "The encampment was regularly laid out," wrote Major William Hull. "The streets ran in parallel lines, neatness and order prevailed, and in viewing it from the hills it had the appearance of a little city."

The huts were not all alike. Soldiers from New England, accustomed to harsh winters, had set their huts in pits three or four feet deep so that the earth would provide a warming blanket of insulation. Southern troops built theirs entirely above ground, which they soon regretted, for the

Washington inspects some of the completed huts.

A reconstructed log hut at Valley Forge. Twelve enlisted men were assigned to each hut. Similar huts for officers had fewer tenants.

huts never seemed warm enough to suit them. All the huts were windowless to keep out the cold. Inside, the men slept side by side on straw mats that had to be replaced often, before they became infested with vermin.

At first, the absence of windows meant that huts became filled with choking smoke when the men burned green wood in their fireplaces. And when it rained, many of the roofs leaked. But once the leaks were plugged and the chimneys adjusted to draw more efficiently, Washington could report that the men were settled in "tolerable good huts."

The small stone house where Washington had set up his headquarters became the busy nerve center of the encampment. The house was crowded at times with twenty or thirty staff officers, messengers, servants, and aides-de-camp, who worked in the office and sitting room next to Washington's office.

Washington drew especially close to two of his aides, who were no older than some of

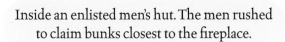

Inside an enlisted men's hut. The men rushed to claim bunks closest to the fireplace.

John Laurens, an aide to General Washington. His father, Henry Laurens, was president of the Continental Congress.

Alexander Hamilton, another young Washington aide and a close friend of John Laurens.
Portrait by Thomas Hamilton Crawford.

the enlisted men. Twenty-three-year-old John Laurens of South Carolina, a brilliant lawyer educated in Switzerland and England, had written to Washington offering to serve "the cause" in any capacity as an unpaid volunteer. He had fought courageously at the battles of Brandywine Creek and Germantown, where he was wounded. His father, Henry Laurens, was president of the Continental Congress. Young John provided a vital link between his influential father and the commander in chief.

Alexander Hamilton of New York was twenty-two. An artillery officer and a hero of Washington's victory at the battle of Princeton, he had dropped out of King's College (now Columbia University) to fight in the Revolutionary War. Hamilton was a quick-witted conversationalist and a skilled writer who helped draft and polish Washington's voluminous correspondence. Washington himself had received only seven or eight years of schooling by a private tutor. He selected educated aides who were capable "Pen-men" with a confident mastery of grammar and sentence construction.

The youngest member of what Washington called his "military family"—and the youngest general in the Continental army—was a

The Marquis de Lafayette, at nineteen the youngest general in the Continental army and the most famous foreign officer to serve with Washington.
From a portrait by Alonzo Chappel.

volunteer from France, the Marquis de Lafayette. This tall, skinny, idealistic, and immensely wealthy nobleman had sailed to America on a ship of his own to offer his services in the cause of liberty. Landing on the coast of South Carolina after evading a British blockade, Lafayette dramatically raised his right hand and swore to live or die for the ideals of the American Revolution.

Lafayette's powerful relatives in France had much influence at the court of Louis XVI. France, a longtime enemy of England, was secretly shipping arms and ammunition to the American rebels. Lafayette had written to Congress, volunteering to serve without pay. Recognizing his valuable family connections in the French court, Congress eagerly gave the nineteen-year-old French aristocrat an honorary appointment as a major general in the Continental army.

At six foot four, Lafayette was one of the few men who could look Washington directly in the eyes. When they first met, Washington invited Lafayette to witness a review of the troops. As the ragged, threadbare Continental army marched past, Washington apologized. "We are rather embarrassed to show ourselves to an officer who has just left the army of France," he said. Lafayette snapped to attention, and without hesitation replied, "I am here, sir, to learn and not to teach."

Though the young Frenchman had no real military experience, he wanted to prove himself in battle. Just five days after Lafayette's twentieth birthday, Washington gave him a minor command at the battle of Brandywine Creek. He performed with coolness and courage, coming to within twenty yards of the enemy, staying on the battlefield despite a painful leg wound, and impressing Washington with his personal bravery. "The Marquis is determined to be in the way of danger," Washington said. As he ordered Lafayette from the field to have his wound dressed, Washington told the surgeon, "Treat him as though he were my son."

Lafayette, Hamilton, and Laurens became the best of friends, their relationship aided by Hamilton's and Laurens's fluency in French. And Washington, who was childless, became a father figure who treated all three of these young men as the sons he had never had. They ate with him at the headquarters house and with Martha when she visited the camp, slept in the upstairs bedrooms, and became an inseparable part of Washington's life.

Lafayette especially formed a close and lasting bond with Washington. Writing to his wife in Paris, who was expecting their first child, Lafayette called Washington "that inestimable man, whose talents and virtues I admire—the better I know him the more I venerate him. . . . I am established in his home, and we live together like two attached brothers, with mutual confidence and cordiality."

Although the troops were no longer freezing in tents, they still could not count on a steady supply of food. The quartermaster and commissary departments, which were supposed to feed and clothe the troops, were disorganized and ineffective. The army's supply system had collapsed.

Early in February, a blizzard lasted for two days and buried the camp in snow. With the shortage of horses, most of which had died of starvation, it was almost impossible to transport and distribute what little food was available. Snow was followed by rising temperatures and heavy rains. When the temperature plunged again, sheets of ice made the roads impassable.

"The situation of the camp is such that in all human probability the army must soon dissolve," General Varnum reported on February 12. Soldiers were deserting the camp in "astonishingly great" numbers, their devotion to the cause overcome "by hunger, the keenest of necessities." Varnum warned that the desperate lack of supplies might "in the end force the army to mutiny."

Washington tried to deal with the food crisis by sending foraging parties deep into the surrounding countryside. Provisions and livestock hidden from the soldiers were confiscated when found. The army required enormous amounts of food. When livestock and wheat were available, the soldiers wolfed down a million pounds of meat and a million pounds of bread a month. "The Country is very much drained," reported Major General Nathanael Greene of Rhode Island, commander of a foraging party. "The inhabitants cry out and beset me from all quarters, but like Pharaoh I harden my heart."

A solution to the food crisis depended on the five congressmen who had arrived in Valley Forge at the end of January. When the politicians saw for themselves the sorry condition of the sickly, hungry troops, they were horrified. Many of the enlisted men were in rags. Officers wore coats "of every color and make." A visitor saw some officers mounting guard wearing "a sort of dressing gown made of old blankets or woolen bedcovers."

The congressmen had heard rumors spread by Washington's critics that he was weak and indecisive, but when they met him, they were impressed by his commanding presence and forthright manner. Far from being indecisive, Washington presented the congressmen with a lengthy report, largely in Alexander Hamilton's handwriting, detailing "the defects in our military system" and suggesting changes designed to solve the army's pressing problems. "Something must be done," the report began. "Important alterations must be made."

Washington urged a complete overhaul of the army's supply system from the top down—a responsibility, he pointed out, that rested with Congress. He offered specific proposals to reorganize the army and to recruit more officers and enlisted men. And he recommended recruiting two or three hundred American Indians as a special scouting unit.

When the politicians first arrived at Valley Forge, the embattled commander in chief had told them, "Congress does not trust me. I cannot continue thus." His detailed report, backed up by what the committee members had seen with their own eyes, erased any doubts about his leadership. "My dear General," one of the congressmen told

Winter scenes at Valley Forge. At bottom left, Washington ponders his problems as his army endures winter hardships. *Illustration by Charles Stanley Reinhart from* Harper's Weekly, *March 1, 1873.*

Washington gives the five-man committee sent by Congress a guided tour of Valley Forge and a close look at his ragged, hungry men.
Engraving, 1866, from a painting by W. H. Powell.

Washington, "if you had given some explanation [to Congress], all these rumors would have been silenced a long time ago."

All along, Washington had recognized how dangerous it would be to reveal his army's weakness to the British. So he had remained silent when he was accused of being timid and ineffectual. "How could I [defend] myself," he asked, "without doing harm to the public cause?"

From then on, he could count on the support of Congress. And as the quartermaster and commissary departments were reorganized under new leadership, the army began to receive adequate supplies of food and clothing.

Meanwhile, Washington let it be known that he had learned the identity of his critics—General Conway and others. And he threw down the gauntlet, challenging them to replace him. "Whenever the public gets dissatisfied with my services," he announced, "or a person is found better qualified . . . I shall quit the helm . . . and retire to private life." With that, the whispering campaign was silenced. Men who had been attacking Washington behind his back fell all over one another claiming to be his warmest admirers.

For the rest of war, Washington's leadership was not seriously challenged. Now he could concentrate on strengthening his army.

SIX

The Secret Agent

WRITING TO HIS WIFE IN PARIS, Lafayette reported: "Several general officers have brought their wives to camp. . . . General Washington has also just decided to send for his wife, a modest and respectable person who loves her husband madly."

Martha Washington left their comfortable home at Mount Vernon in the beginning of 1778 and made the long journey north across ice-choked rivers and frozen winter roads. She reached Valley Forge on February 10, arriving by sleigh over the snowdrifts. It was the third year that she had joined her husband at camp, and as she made her appearance, she was cheered by the troops.

She would spend the rest of the winter with "the general," as she often called George, who towered over his plump, four-foot-eleven-inch, adoring wife. "Mrs. Washington is extremely fond of the general and he of her," observed an officer's wife. "They are very happy in each other."

Martha Dandridge Custis, known to friends as "Patsy," at the age of twenty-six—two years before her marriage to George Washington. *Portrait, 1757, by John Wollaston.*

Martha immediately took charge of the meals, such as they were, and insisted that a log cabin be built as a dining room adjoining the headquarters house. "The General's apartment is very small," she told a friend. "He has had a log cabin built to dine in which has made our quarter[s] much more tolerable than they were."

High-ranking officers and important visitors took for granted an open invitation to share food and drink with the commander in chief at his headquarters. Often there were fifteen or twenty men, along with an occasional officer's wife, assembled at Washington's table for a simple midday dinner. The general's guests would sit at the table for two or three hours after the meal, munching nuts, sipping Madeira wine, discussing the day's events, and planning strategies for the future.

Martha, a talkative, generous, kindly woman with tiny hands and feet, did what she could to aid the troops and boost their morale. She visited soldiers in their huts and at

An artist's impression of the formal courtship between George and Martha. She was a wealthy Virginia widow, and he was a young hero of the French and Indian War.

the camp hospital, spreading good cheer and encouragement, pretending not to notice the stench of decaying horse carcasses and open latrines. And she organized a sewing circle of officers' wives who gathered every morning to knit socks, sew shirts, and patch trousers for needy soldiers.

Occasionally, George and Martha invited officers and their wives to a social evening in the candlelit sitting room of the headquarters house. Washington had a chance to relax at these informal gatherings. He became a "chatty, agreeable companion," an officer's wife told a friend, and apparently something of a flirt "who can be downright impudent sometimes, such impudence, Fanny, as you and I like."

"In the midst of all our distresses, there were some bright sides to the picture," another guest recalled. "The evening was spent in conversation over a dish of tea or coffee. There was no . . . dancing, card-playing, or amusements of any kind, except singing. Every gentleman or lady who could sing was called upon in turn for a song."

Songs and music were popular forms of diversion at Valley Forge. One evening just before Christmas, Dr. Albigence Waldo was walking past a soldiers' tent when he heard "an excellent player on the violin" whose plaintive melody was "so finely adapted to stir up the tenderest passions." The hardships of the winter camp were forgotten for the moment. As the violinist played, the music called up for Waldo fond memories of "all the endearing expressions, the tender sentiments, the sympathetic friendship . . . of the tenderest of the fair . . . I wished to have the music cease and yet dreaded its ceasing lest I should lose sight of those dear ideas which gave me pain and pleasure at the same time."

A French interpreter at the camp was similarly moved while walking in the woods before breakfast one morning. From a distance he heard "a most powerful voice . . . yet melodious," singing a song from a popular French opera. He was astonished "when suddenly I saw . . . before me a tall Indian . . . in American regimentals and two large epaulets on his shoulders." The singer was a Canadian Abenaki who spoke French and

Cricket as played in the 1770s—a popular sport at Valley Forge.

The enlisted men also held boxing and wrestling matches. *Illustration, 1796, by C. R. Ryley.*

English. Raised by Jesuit priests under French rule in Canada, he had joined the Americans at the beginning of the war, rising to the rank of colonel in the Continental army.

Soldiers in their tents and huts had all sorts of simple, handmade musical instruments, such as tin whistles and Jews' harps, which are held between the teeth and plucked to produce a soft, twanging sound. In their spare time, the men played cards, shot marbles, and read. When the weather allowed, they held footraces and outdoor boxing and wrestling matches. And they organized team sports like wicket, a version of cricket, and "base," an early forerunner of baseball.

Officers rehearsed and acted in the popular plays of the day. They gave dinner parties at which the guests shared their food rations. A French volunteer remembered one dinner party to which no one was admitted who possessed a complete set of trousers. "Torn clothes were an indispensable requisite for admission," he wrote, "and in this the guests were very sure not to fail . . . . Such a ragged and at the same time merry set of fellows were never before brought together."

On the morning of Sunday, February 22, 1778, Washington was at work in his office when an artillery band of fifers and drummers marched to the snow-covered field in front of the headquarters house and serenaded their commander on his forty-sixth birthday. It was the first public recognition of George Washington's birthday, an event that Americans have been celebrating ever since.

German-born General Friedrich von Steuben makes his first appearance at Valley Forge. *From a painting by Alonzo Chappel.*

Another visitor to Valley Forge that February was a stout, balding German gentleman with a shady past. Riding into camp with his four aides and a large Russian wolfhound named Azor, he announced himself as Lieutenant General Friedrich Wilhelm August Heinrich Ferdinand Baron von Steuben. A professional soldier in the Prussian army, and a veteran of several European campaigns, he had served as an aide to Frederick the Great, the king of Prussia.

The baron had volunteered to serve the rebel cause without rank or pay. "My greatest ambition," he had written to Washington, "is to render your country all the services in my power and to deserve the title of a citizen of America by fighting for the cause of your liberty." Washington greeted him on the outskirts of the Valley Forge encampment. "The Baron Steuben has arrived in camp," he reported. "He appears to be much of a gentleman, and as far as I have had an opportunity of judging, a man of military knowledge and acquainted with the world."

The day after Steuben arrived, the troops were mustered for his review. "When I looked on the baron," one private remembered, "he seemed to me a perfect personification of Mars [the god of war]." That soldier would never forget the "trappings of [Steuben's] horse, the enormous holsters of his pistols, his large size, and his strikingly martial aspect."

With his imposing military bearing, jovial manner, and booming voice, Steuben impressed everyone. But he was not quite the person he claimed to be. He wasn't really a lieutenant general. The highest rank he had ever held was that of captain. Even so, he had an extensive knowledge of European military procedures and a passion for drilling troops on the parade ground.

Steuben was, in fact, an unemployed soldier of fortune who had sailed to America as a secret agent of the French government. The French had been aiding the American rebels with money, arms, and volunteers. But they were concerned that the Continental army lacked the conventional military skills that would enable it to stand up against a disciplined foreign army in open battle.

Steuben was an experienced drillmaster. His mission was to mold the rebels into a professional fighting force trained in the European manner. French officials in Paris had invented Steuben's rank and titles and sent him off to America as a "volunteer." Benjamin Franklin, the American ambassador to France, had helped engineer the scheme, and Steuben, a born actor, played his role with gusto and conviction.

The Continental army had been founded by Congress less than three years earlier. So far, the army's training had been sketchy and haphazard. There were no uniform standards of march or maneuver. Every regiment followed a different system of drill. Each man handled his weapon in his own way. "Our arms are in horrible condition," reported a committee of officers, "covered with rust, half of them without bayonets, many from which not a single shot can be fired. . . . Muskets, carbines, fowling pieces and rifles are to be seen in the same Company."

Washington and Steuben reviewing the troops.

An illustration by John Andrew from Ballou's Pictorial, September 13, 1856.

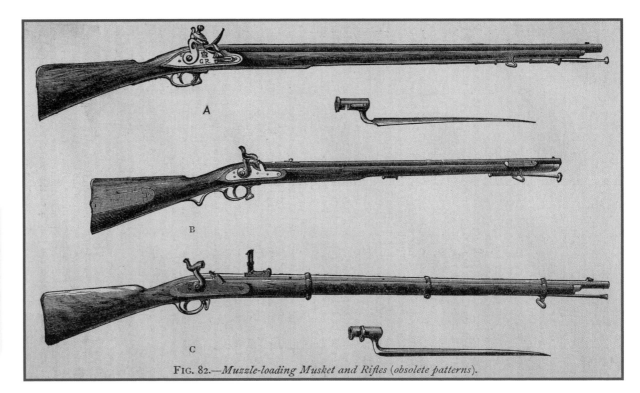

FIG. 82.—*Muzzle-loading Musket and Rifles (obsolete patterns).*

Musket and rifles around 1800. At top, the British-made "Brown Bess" musket and bayonet, used widely by the Americans early in the war. Below, two British rifles. American rifles were accurate at long range but could not be equipped with bayonets.

The standard infantry weapon of the time was the quick-loading, single-shot musket, called a firelock because it spit out a flash of fire when discharged. The English-made "Brown Bess" musket, used extensively by the Americans early in the war, was three-and-a-half feet long and weighed fourteen pounds. Later it was replaced by lighter and stronger French muskets. A musket had to be reloaded after each shot, a complicated process that a trained soldier could complete in twenty seconds or less as enemy bullets flew around him.

American-made rifles were highly accurate at long distances, much to the sorrow of British soldiers who thought they were safely out of range. But rifles at the time were comparatively slow-loading after each shot and could not be equipped with bayonets, so they weren't much use in close combat. Muskets, however, were accurate only to about eighty yards. As a result, European troops were trained to maneuver and fight in close formation, bringing massive firepower to bear at close range before charging with fixed bayonets.

Most Americans had no experience with this kind of conventional eighteenth-century warfare. They knew how to fight behind stockades and other defensive barriers, how to disperse in the woods, how to wage war against Indians, but they had never before had to perform quickly and efficiently the maneuvers necessary for formal battle of army against army in open country—advancing in formation and firing on command.

Steuben recognized at the outset that American troops were not at all like their European counterparts. For one thing, he doubted that any European army would have

Charging with fixed bayonets—a common tactic of eighteenth-century warfare. *From a painting by John Trumbull.*

held together under similar hardships. And he understood that the Americans were individualists who would not bend to the blind obedience demanded of European soldiers.

"The genius of this nation," Steuben wrote to a friend in Europe, "is not in the least to be compared with that of the Prussians, Austrians, or French. You say to your soldier, 'Do this,' and he doeth it, but I am obliged to say, 'This is the reason that you ought to do that,' and then he does it."

As an example to the other officers, Steuben formed a model company, which he drilled himself. He drilled the troops again and again in different formations, taught them how to aim their muskets, which improved their accuracy, how to charge with a bayonet, and how to maneuver in disciplined compact ranks rather than advancing in long, straggling files. His objective was to train the men to execute orders instantly, to march and maneuver with precision and confidence on a drill field or on the battlefield. Steuben was also a stickler for cleanliness. He expected the men to be neat and shaved, and even if they were wearing rags, those should be clean too.

Steuben spoke little English when he arrived at Valley Forge. He relied on his secretary

Shouting and cursing in fractured English, much to the amusement of the troops, Steuben drills a company of Continental army soldiers.
From a painting by Edwin Abbey.

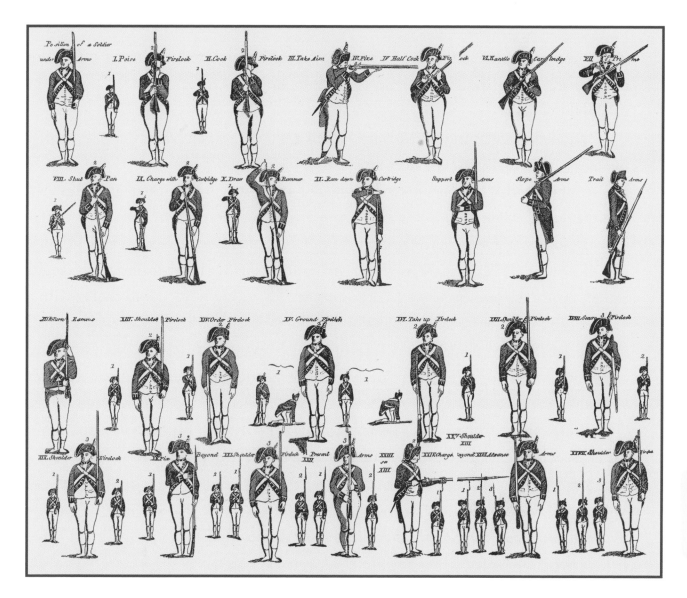

Illustration from an 1802 American manual of arms, showing the drill exercises of the Continental soldiers.

and translator, a seventeen-year-old French nobleman named Pierre Duponceau. On the drill field, Steuben shouted marching orders in fractured English studded with choice German profanities. "When some movement or maneuver was not performed to his [satisfaction]," Duponceau recalled, "he began to swear in German, then in French, and then in both languages together. When he had exhausted his artillery of foreign oaths, he would call to his aides . . . [to] 'come and swear for me in English. These fellows won't do what I bid them." A good-natured smile then went through the ranks and at last the maneuver or the movement was properly performed."

When the troops performed well, Steuben would glow with satisfaction. But when they fumbled, when mistakes were made, he would fly into an hysterical rage, which the soldiers came to expect and heartily enjoy. His "fits of passion were comical and rather amused than offended the soldiers," Duponceau wrote. Steuben became a celebrity at Valley Forge. Drilling with him was now the camp's favorite sport, as different units began to compete with one another. Officers and enlisted men came from all over the camp to stand on the sidelines and watch as he tirelessly drilled, cursed, and drilled again a growing number of Continentals.

Within a few weeks, Steuben transformed the Continental army into a disciplined and efficient European-style fighting force. Finally, American troops could compete on equal terms with British regulars. "My enterprise succeeded better than I had dared to expect," he boasted.

Washington recognized the German drillmaster's accomplishment by appointing him inspector general of the Continental army. "The Importance of establishing a uniform system of useful maneuvers, and regularity of discipline, must be obvious," Washington wrote. Congress approved the appointment and gave Steuben the rank of major general—one rank lower than lieutenant general, which he pretended to have held in the Prussian army, but a big promotion up from captain.

Meanwhile, in cooperation with American officers, Steuben wrote a simplified drill manual titled *Regulations for the Order and Discipline of the Troops of the United States*, popularly known as "The Blue Book." It remained the official source of procedures for training American troops until the War of 1812.

Steuben's reforms came none too soon. With winter ending, the likelihood of a British attack against Valley Forge was now greater than ever.

SEVEN

A Great Day for General Washington

THE LONG WINTER AT VALLEY FORGE was at last coming to an end. As the days grew warmer, soldiers who had been severely tested felt a sense of pride and a new spirit of optimism. Washington praised the way his men had endured "such uncommon hardships . . . bearing them with patience and fortitude."

The starving time was over. Washington had appointed one of his best generals, Nathanael Greene, as the new quartermaster general. Greene accepted reluctantly. Proud of his combat record, he wanted no part of the new job. "No body ever heard of a quarter Master in History," he complained. Even so, he began to correct the army's supply problems, taking command of the disorganized quartermaster's department with the no-nonsense authority of a battlefield commander.

General Nathanael Greene, one of Washington's most capable battlefield commanders. Washington chose him to reform the army's quartermaster department.
From a portrait by John Trumbull.

By April, the revitalized quartermaster and commissary departments were delivering ample food and clothing, including some uniforms for the summer campaign. Congress was about to provide bonuses for enlisted men, along with increased pay and pensions for officers. As a result, fresh troops were marching in, boosting the army's strength. Morale had never been higher.

Washington had been expecting a full-scale British attack. But the only military actions during the winter and early spring were brief clashes with British patrols on the outskirts of Philadelphia. The biggest skirmish took place at the Crooked Billet Tavern, where Pennsylvania militiamen commanded by Brigadier General John Lacey had set up an outpost seventeen miles from the occupied American capital.

Alerted by a spy, a British strike force set out in the predawn darkness of May 1. Redcoats surrounded the American outpost and attacked at daylight, catching the sleeping militiamen by surprise. "The alarm was so sudden," Lacey reported later, "I had scarcely time to mount my horse before the enemy was within musket shot of my quarters." Staggering from their tents, the panicking rebels were trampled by charging British horsemen and bayoneted by the advancing light infantry. Lacey managed to lead an orderly retreat, but more than a hundred American men were killed, wounded, or taken prisoner.

By the time Washington learned about the fight at the Crooked Billet, a courier had galloped into the Valley Forge encampment bearing sensational news from France. Earlier that year, the King of France, Louis XVI, had recognized the independence of the United States. Treaties of friendship and alliance between the two countries had been signed on February 6. News of the alliance, dispatched from Paris and carried across the Atlantic by sailing ship, had taken weeks to reach Valley Forge.

An official notice of the French alliance was delivered to Washington at his headquarters on a spring afternoon. "I believe no event was ever received with more heartfelt joy," he exclaimed in a letter to Henry Laurens. Lafayette was so excited by the news that

Louis XVI, king of France from 1774 to 1792. French aid was crucial to the American defeat of Great Britain. In 1793, following the outbreak of the French Revolution, Louis and his queen, Marie Antoinette, were executed.

In this French engraving
from the 1780s,
George Washington holds
copies of the Declaration
of Independence and the treaty
of alliance with France.
At his feet lie torn copies of
documents relating to British
attempts at reconciliation
with the American colonies.

he burst into Washington's office, embraced his commander in chief, and kissed him in the French fashion on both cheeks.

May 1—May Day—was a traditional holiday that celebrated the end of winter. Bands of soldiers wearing flowers in their hats paraded to fifes and drums past festive Maypoles erected by every regiment. Washington joined in, grinning widely and swinging a cricket bat in a game with a group of young artillery officers. The commander in chief, said Ensign George Ewing, "did us the honor to play at wicket with us."

With the French alliance, the war entered a new phase. France had been secretly supporting the American rebels with arms, money, and volunteers since the summer of 1776. Now the powerful French navy, stationed in the West Indies, could challenge the British naval supremacy along American shores. And if France joined with Spain and other European nations to oppose England, then the British might have to abandon the war in America. "Be very sure," warned British statesman Edmund Burke, "this country [England] is incapable of carrying on a war with America and these [other] powers acting in conjunction."

An official day of "public celebration" took place on May 6, when the entire Continental army turned out for inspection and a grand parade. The morning began with the booming of a cannon as the soldiers assembled to hear the good news proclaimed and their chaplains offer grateful thanks for the French alliance. Then a second cannon boomed. Rank by rank, each battalion paraded past General Washington and his staff, then deployed into a double line of battle. The commander in chief passed down the lines, reviewing the spruced-up troops who stood smartly at attention, their bayonets polished and glinting in the morning sun.

This army was dramatically different from the ragtag troops Lafayette had first reviewed a year before. An officer praised "the air of our soldiers, the cleanliness of their dress, the brilliance and good order of their arms, and the remarkable animation with which they performed the necessary salute as the General passed along. Indeed, during

Reviewing the
Continental army
troops. *From an 1885
painting by Henry
Alexander Ogden.*

the whole of the review, the utmost military decorum was preserved, while at the same time one might observe the hearts of the soldiers struggling to express their feelings."

Now cannons boomed thirteen times, saluting each of the thirteen united states, followed by what the French call a *feu de joie*, a joyful firing of arms. One after another, the men in the first line raised their muskets and fired. Blasts of smoke and sound moved down the line in swift succession, then ran up the second line with military precision. The thundering cannon and rhythmic firing of arms, "swelling and rebounding from the neighboring hills and gently sweeping along the Schuylkill" mingled with the cheers of thousands of troops as their commanders shouted, "Long live France!" "Long live the friendly powers!" "Long live the American states!" "Their voices," wrote one enthusiastic soldier, "composed a military music more agreeable to a soldier's ear" than the most beautiful music "of your favorite Handel."

When the ceremonies ended, enlisted men scattered across the sprawling encampment to play wicket and pitch balls, while George and Martha Washington greeted officers and their wives at a festive outdoor banquet. "Fifteen hundred people sat down to the tables, which were spread in the open air," General de Kalb recalled. "All the officers with their ladies. . . . Wine, meats, and liquors abounded, and happiness and contentment were impressed on every countenance. Numberless hurrahs were given for the King of France. . . . It was a fine day for us, and a great one for General Washington. Let me say that no one could be more worthy of this good fortune."

Late that afternoon, as George and Martha stood to take their leave, everyone broke into applause and "loud huzzas, which continued till Washington had proceeded a quarter of a mile, during which time there were a thousand hats tossed in the air. His Excellency turned round with his retinue and huzzaed several times."

Back at his headquarters, Washington was in the highest of spirits. He wrote optimistically to a friend that "those dark and tempestuous clouds which at times appeared ready to overwhelm us" might now be passing. For the first time, he looked forward to an early and victorious ending to the war.

The occupation of Philadelphia had given the British a snug winter retreat but little military advantage. "The possession of our Towns, while we have an Army in the field, will avail them little," Washington had predicted. British sorties into the countryside had met with determined resistance from rebel militiamen. And the feared British offensive against Valley Forge had never materialized—at least not yet. General William Howe, the cautious British commander, had not attempted to attack the strongly fortified encampment.

With the Continental army's new allies, training, and spirit, driving the British from Philadelphia seemed only a matter of time. "To us who had built ourselves a city on the banks of the Schuylkill, the return of spring brought thoughts of happiness, which we should have enjoyed more fully, were Philadelphia again our possession," Lieutenant James McMichael wrote in his diary. "We rely on the prudence and military skill of our worthy General to accomplish this."

Lafayette, Washington, and Steuben at Valley Forge. Icicles hang from the roofs of log huts in the background. Lafayette as pictured here looks considerably older than he actually was at the time. The artist may have had only a later portrait of Lafayette to use as a reference. *From an 1894 book illustration by A. Tholey.*

General William Howe, (above) who failed to destroy the American army, was replaced as British commander in chief by Sir Henry Clinton (below).

Taking Back Philadelphia

WASHINGTON'S SPIES reported that a new British commander was on his way to Philadelphia. General William Howe, who had let the winter pass without attacking Valley Forge, would be sailing back home to London. Howe was being replaced by General Henry Clinton, commander of the British forces occupying New York.

Washington summoned his fellow generals to a council of war. Now that France had entered the war, what would Clinton do? Would he keep the British forces hunkered down in occupied Philadelphia? Would he mount an all-out offensive against Valley Forge? Rumors hinted that Clinton was expecting thousands of additional troops as reinforcements.

For the time being, Washington and his generals decided to stay on at Valley Forge. They would watch for any enemy move and continue to strengthen the Continental army, which was fast gaining new recruits. The main army at Valley Forge now numbered nearly 12,000 men. Another 3,000 were stationed in the New York Highlands and at Wilmington, Delaware. With expected reinforcements, Washington would have perhaps 20,000 troops under his command.

By now, fresh uniforms were arriving and the troops were at last eating well. Writing to his fiancée, Phebe, Major Samuel Ward Jr. of Rhode Island reported that the enlisted men had begun to "grow healthy as the fine season approaches." As for himself, at dinnertime the major enjoyed "a piece of good beef or pork tho generally of both—and have as good bread as I ever eat," along with plenty of tea, coffee, milk, and sugar.

During the winter, a group of officers who called themselves Washington's Strolling Players had put on a couple of plays before small audiences crowded into the bakehouse, where the army's bread was made. Washington loved the theater and before the war had attended plays often. Now that spring had arrived, he had his engineers build a large outdoor theater on the banks of the Schuylkill, where the Strolling Players staged more plays. Officers and their wives filled the seats in the audience, while enlisted men gathered at the rear of the open-air theater, where they could watch the action even when they could not hear the actors.

As the days grew warmer, the enlisted men's windowless huts became unbearably hot. And with twelve men who had little chance to bathe crowded into each hut, the log cabins began to stink. To let in fresh air, Washington ordered two windows cut into the walls of each hut. Later, the hardened mud between the logs was chipped away to help improve air circulation. Eventually, the soldiers moved out of the smelly huts and back into airy tents.

Washington's spies were now reporting that General Clinton, the new British commander, was planning to evacuate his forces from Philadelphia. Even if the reports were true, there was still the danger that Clinton might order an all-out attack against Valley Forge. Washington dispatched 2,200 troops commanded by Lafayette on a reconnaissance mission to find out what the British were up to. Lafayette's force included forty-

An American rifleman. While fresh uniforms began to arrive at Valley Forge, the Americans never presented the polished appearance of the British and French. The Continental Congress had little money to equip the troops, and the individual states supplied uniforms of various styles and colors.

seven Oneida Indian scouts, "stout-looking fellows and remarkably neat," according to Private Joseph Plumb Martin, who was assigned to the expedition. The Oneidas had adopted Lafayette into their tribe and named him Kayweda, after one of their greatest warriors.

On May 18, Lafayette established a base camp at Barren Hill, about twelve miles from Philadelphia and just a couple of miles from the nearest British outposts. Two mornings later, as a low fog hung over the American camp, a surprise British assault almost trapped the young French general and his troops. "We were told that the British were advancing upon us in our rear," Martin recalled. "How they could get there was to us a mystery, but they *were* there."

Lafayette led his troops on a rapid retreat to the Schuylkill River, about three miles away. "The enemy had nearly surrounded us by the time our retreat commenced," Martin wrote, "but the road we were on was very favorable for us, it being for the most part ... through small woods and copses. ... We crossed the Schuylkill in good order. ... As fast as the troops crossed they formed and prepared for action, and waited for them to attack us. But we saw no more of them that time, for before we had reached the river the alarm guns were fired in our camp and the whole [American] army was immediately in motion. The British, fearing that they should be outnumbered in their turn, directly set their faces for Philadelphia and set off in as much or more haste than we had left Barren Hill."

At Valley Forge, lookouts atop watchtowers had spotted the retreating Americans and alerted the alarm guns. In less than five minutes, thanks to Steuben's training, Washington had his whole army under arms and ready to march to Lafayette's aid. Steuben's drills also enabled Lafayette's troops to execute their swift and orderly retreat, moving quickly in a compact body to a ford at the Schuylkill. If they had been strung out along the road, many of the troops would have been cut off by the British and captured or killed.

This idealized portrait of Lafayette leading his troops was painted by Edward Percy Moran around 1909. Lafayette was, in fact, a daring battlefield commander. At the Battle of Brandywine, he was wounded in the leg.

The Oneida scouts, bringing up the rear of the retreating American column, made their own contribution to Lafayette's escape. As British cavalrymen brandishing sabers galloped toward the retreating Americans, the Oneidas let loose with a hair-raising war whoop, startling the horsemen and frightening their steeds. The horses bolted and turned heel, giving the Americans time to reach the river safely. Later, when the British began their own retreat, the Oneidas rushed back across the river and harassed the enemy's flanks as the redcoats hurried toward Philadelphia.

After that, Washington relied on his network of spies to keep an eye on the British. Some of his best spies were washerwomen who did laundry for British officials in Philadelphia. In June, they reported that the officials had ordered their laundry delivered at once, "finished or unfinished." It appeared that a British evacuation was about to begin.

General Clinton, the British commander, had learned that a French fleet was on its way to America and would arrive any day. Clinton decided to evacuate Philadelphia before French warships could blockade the city's harbor and trap the redcoats occupying the city. He would concentrate his forces at New York.

Most of the British cavalry and artillery was loaded aboard transport ships crowding the Philadelphia harbor and ferried to New York by sea. The ships also carried some 3,000 Loyalists—Americans who had sworn an oath of allegiance to King George and were now desperate refugees, many with children, and all with piles of baggage. The rest of Clinton's army, some 9,000 troops, with a baggage train of 1,500 wagons that stretched out for twelve miles, prepared to march overland across New Jersey to New York.

On June 18, fifteen minutes after the last British detachment left Philadelphia, American cavalry troops galloped triumphantly into the city, taking back the American capital. The same day, Washington sent out advance units to nip at the heels of the retreating British troops and harass their rear columns.

The next morning—at 5 A.M. on June 19, 1778—General George Washington, tall in the saddle, led the rest of the Continental army out of Valley Forge. These men bore little resemblance to the freezing, starving troops who had arrived at the winter camp six months earlier to the day. With the aid of a possessed German drillmaster, and with his own steely determination, Washington had transformed his cavalcade of wild beasts into a disciplined professional fighting force ready to meet the British on the field of battle.

Marching in orderly formation, keeping step to the rhythm and beat of fife and drum, their regimental colors flying brightly overhead, the soldiers of the Continental army left behind the humble log huts that had sheltered them during the winter at Valley Forge—huts that were empty now and would never be occupied again.

Boats and ships along the waterfront of Philadelphia, the largest and wealthiest city in America at the time of the Revolution. British troops occupying the city evacuated on June 18, 1778.
A German engraving from the 1770s.

NINE

"Band of Brothers"

———•———

NINE DAYS after marching away from Valley Forge, Washington's newly trained army had a chance to prove itself in battle. Advance units had trailed the redcoats into New Jersey, sniping at their rear guard. On June 28, 1778, the main Continental army caught up with the British near the village of Monmouth Court House (now Freehold) and launched a full-scale attack.

The forces clashed amid smoke and confusion on a sweltering day—attacking and counterattacking, pushing forward and falling back. When one of Washington's generals ordered his men to retreat, Washington galloped across the field in a towering rage, swearing "till the leaves shook on the trees," and took command of the situation himself. It was "a day that would have made any man swear," Brigadier General Charles Scott recalled. "Never have I enjoyed such swearing before or since. Sir, on that ever-memorable day, he swore like an angel from Heaven."

Later, Washington was seen rallying his troops while sitting calmly astride his white

Washington, on horseback, rallies his troops at the Battle of Monmouth.
Engraving, 1858, from a book illustration by Felix O. C. Darley.

charger as British artillery shells tore up the earth all around him. Alexander Hamilton reported that he "never saw the general to such an advantage. His coolness and firmness were admirable."

"Molly Pitcher,"
the legendary heroine
of Monmouth.
*Hand-colored lithograph published
by Currier and Ives.*

During the height of the battle, a woman named Mary Ludwig Hayes, who was carrying pitchers of water to the troops from a nearby spring, took her husband's place loading the muzzle of a cannon after he was overcome by heat. She seemed unfazed when a British cannonball came whistling over the field and passed right between her legs.

No less an authority than Private Joseph Plumb Martin wrote later that he was an eyewitness to this scene: "While in the act of reaching [for] a cartridge and having one of her feet as far before the other as she could step, a cannon shot from the enemy passed directly between her legs without doing any other damage than carrying away all the lower part of her petticoat. Looking at it with apparent unconcern, she continued her occupation."

When the battle ended, Mary Hayes continued to carry pitcher after pitcher of water to the wounded, earning the nickname "Molly Pitcher," by which she has been known ever since.

The Battle of Monmouth continued all day under a broiling sun, with each side taking then giving up patches of ground. Scores of men on both sides were killed or wounded. Others collapsed on the field and died of heatstroke. "It was almost impossible to breathe," Private Martin remembered.

At one point during the fighting, Martin fired his musket at a line of retreating redcoats: "I singled out a man and took my aim directly between his shoulders. He was a good mark, being a broad-shouldered fellow. What became of him I know not; the fire and smoke hid him from my sight. One thing I know, that is, I took as deliberate aim at him as ever I did at any game in my life. But after all, I hope I did not kill him, although I intended to at the time."

At dusk, the fading light brought the fighting to an end. Washington spread his cloak on the ground and slept among his troops. During the night, the battered British forces managed to slip away under cover of darkness and hightail it for New York.

While the British escaped to fight another day, Monmouth was called a victory by

American newspapers, by Congress, and by the elated Continental troops themselves, who had proven that they could hold their own against seasoned British regulars in open battle.

In terms of strength, the two armies were evenly matched, with about 13,000 troops on each side—making this the largest one-day battle of the war. Monmouth was also the last major action to take place in the North. Afterward, fighting shifted to the southern colonies, where Americans led by General Nathanael Greene carried on a campaign of hit-and-run guerrilla warfare, gradually wearing down British strength. "We fight, get beat, rise and fight again," Greene told a friend.

The climactic battle of the war took place in 1781, when British regulars commanded by Lord Charles Cornwallis marched into Virginia and took a stand at Yorktown. By then, French warships and troops had joined with the main American army under

Washington inspects French artillery batteries in the trenches at Yorktown.
Drawing by Rufus F. Zogbaum from Harper's Weekly, *October 22, 1881.*

General Washington and were converging on Virginia. Outnumbered and outflanked, Cornwallis and his redcoats found themselves trapped on the York peninsula, between the French-American forces facing them and the York River at their backs.

American troops storm a British fortification outside Yorktown. An assault such as this almost always ended in hand-to-hand combat.

The siege of Yorktown, punctuated by tremendous artillery barrages and infantry assaults against British fortifications, lasted for three weeks. Washington, as was his habit, put himself in the thick of the fighting. During an attack on an enemy outpost, the general and two of his staff officers had dismounted and were standing on the battlefield, exposed to British cannon and musketry fire. An aide, fearful for Washington's safety, told him, "Sir, you are too much exposed here. Had you not better step back a little bit?"

"Colonel Cobb," Washington replied, "if you are afraid, you have the liberty to step back."

On October 19, 1781, the British surrendered to Washington at Yorktown—a spectacular triumph for the Americans and their French allies. General Cornwallis could not bring himself to hand over his sword to Washington in person. Pleading illness, he excused himself from the surrender ceremony and delegated his second in command, General Charles O'Hara, to surrender on his behalf.

On that warm October afternoon, the combined French-American army, bands playing, marched out to a broad plain behind Yorktown and assembled in two lines that stretched more than a mile in length, the Americans on one side of the road, the French on the other. The French troops looked splendid in their brilliant white-and-blue uniforms. The Americans seemed drab by comparison, some wearing their fringed hunting shirts, others in worn uniforms of various styles, yet they stood proud and erect, beaming with satisfaction and joy. Meanwhile, thousands of spectators from the surrounding countryside had gathered to watch the day's ceremonies.

Surrender at Yorktown:
British General Charles O'Hara,
acting for the absent
Lord Cornwallis, approaches
Washington on his white charger,
ready to hand over his sword.

*Engraving, 1879, from a painting
by A. B. Frost (Arthur Burdett).*

General O'Hara, acting for Lord Cornwallis, rode onto the field at the head of the defeated British troops, who followed with a slow and solemn step as they marched along the road between the rows of Americans and French. Bystanders noticed that many of the redcoats walked unsteadily and "appeared to be much in liquor," having raided all the alcohol they could find in Yorktown.

O'Hara, possibly confused, tried to present his sword to the French commander, the Comte de Rochambeau. But Rochambeau refused to accept it. The French army, he said, was subordinate to the Americans "on this continent." He waved his hand and pointed to Washington.

O'Hara hesitated. Then he steered his horse over to Washington, who sat calmly astride his great white charger. After six years of war, Washington would insist on the deference due him as the victorious commander. The ritual of surrender must be played out according to the rules. As O'Hara offered his sword a second time, Washington also refused to accept it. He instructed O'Hara to present the sword to General Benjamin Lincoln, Washington's second in command and the equivalent of O'Hara in rank.

When the surrender sword was finally handed over and accepted, the British troops were ordered to march to the center of the field, one regiment at a time, and lay down their arms. Some of the redcoats slammed their muskets violently onto the growing pile of weapons, as if determined to break the firing mechanisms and prevent their future use. One man, a corporal, embraced his musket, then threw it on the ground, exclaiming, "May you never get so good a master again!"

According to the custom of the time, British officers were allowed to keep their sidearms. They seemed as sullen and dejected as their men. "In general [they] behaved like boys who had been whipped at school," observed an American officer who was present that day. "Some bit their lips, some pouted, others cried. Their round, broad-brimmed hats were well adapted to the occasion, hiding those faces they were ashamed to show."

The Americans were jubilant. That evening, a colonel recalled, "I noticed that the [American] officers and soldiers could scarcely talk for laughing, and they could scarcely walk for jumping and dancing and singing as they went about."

Although Washington couldn't know it at the time, Yorktown would be the last major battle of the Revolutionary War. After two more years of skirmishes and diplomatic negotiations, Great Britain and the United States signed the Treaty of Paris on September 3, 1783, formally recognizing American independence.

Washington's triumphal entry into New York City following the British evacuation, November 25, 1783. *Lithograph, 1879, by Edmund P. and Ludwig Restein.*

✳ ✳ ✳

From the opening shots at Lexington and Concord to the ceremonial signing of the Treaty of Paris, the American War of Independence lasted nearly eight and a half years. The turning point came when the Continental army survived the winter at Valley Forge and emerged tested and toughened as an effective fighting force.

Writing from Valley Forge on March 9, 1778, Washington's aide John Laurens told his father, Henry, "I would cherish those dear ragged Continentals whose patience will be the admiration of future ages, and glory in bleeding with them." Three months after sending that letter, John had his horse shot out from under him at the Battle of Monmouth. Later he challenged General Charles Lee to a duel, accusing Lee of attacking George Washington's character. Lee suffered a slight bullet wound in the side. Laurens was unhurt.

During the rest of the war, Laurens served as a special diplomatic envoy to France, as Washington's spokesman during surrender negotiations at Yorktown, and as commander of an infantry regiment in the South. He survived four battle wounds, spent six months as a prisoner of war, and won a reputation for reckless courage. In August 1782, with the war nearing its end, Laurens was shot from the saddle during a minor skirmish in South Carolina. He died of his wounds at the age of twenty-seven.

Alexander Hamilton distinguished himself as Washington's chief aide and as a fierce and brilliant field commander. At Yorktown he led an infantry attack alongside French troops, capturing a key enemy fortification and forcing the British to surrender. After the war, Hamilton was one of three authors of the *Federalist Papers,* a series of eighty-five influential articles written to convince New York voters to approve the United States Constitution. He became President George Washington's secretary of the treasury, helped write Washington's farewell speech, and had much influence over the new nation's economic, foreign, and military policies. Hamilton was shot and killed in a duel with his political rival Aaron Burr on July 12, 1804. He was either forty-seven or forty-nine when he died—his birth date in the British West Indies is uncertain.

George Washington as he appeared at the Constitutional Convention in Philadelphia, four years after the Revolutionary War ended. *Painted and engraved in 1787 by Charles Willson Peale.*

"Band of Brothers"

U.S. postage stamp
honoring Lafayette
on the two-hundredth
anniversary of
his birth.

The Marquis de Lafayette commanded troops at Monmouth, Yorktown, and other battles. After the war, he kept up a lifelong friendship and correspondence with Washington. He named his son Georges Washington Lafayette and asked Washington to be the child's godfather. Back in Europe, Lafayette played a leading role in the French Revolution, was arrested during the Reign of Terror, and spent five years in prison. After his release, he remained active in French politics until his death on May 20, 1834, at the age of seventy-six. During World War I, when American expeditionary forces landed in Europe as allies of France, they announced as a tribute to Lafayette's service to America: "Lafayette, we are here!"

The Baron Friedrich von Steuben commanded one of the three divisions of Washington's army at the siege of Yorktown. The last letter Washington wrote before resigning as commander in chief was to Steuben, thanking him for his services to the Continental army. After the war, Steuben became an American citizen. He settled in upstate New York, served as an elder in the German Reformed Church, and lived quietly as a lifelong bachelor on a pension awarded by Congress at a 16,000-acre estate near Utica granted to him by New York State. He died in Steubenville, New York, on November 28, 1794, at the age of sixty-four. His estate is now the Steuben Memorial State Historic Site, a public park.

Joseph Plumb Martin fought at Monmouth, Yorktown, and numerous other battles as a private in the Eighth Connecticut Regiment. After the war he settled in Prospect, Maine. He became a farmer and carpenter, married eighteen-year-old Lucy Clewly, built a big house on Penobscot Bay, and raised five children. He was known for miles around as a popular yarn-spinning veteran of the Revolutionary War. Though he had never attended school, he was an avid reader and self-taught writer, and at the urging of friends, he wrote an account of his service in the Continental army. It was published anonymously in 1830 under the title A *Narrative of Some of the Adventures, Dangers and Sufferings of a Revolutionary Soldier, Interspersed with Anecdotes of Incidents That Occurred*

Washington at Valley Forge

Within His Own Observation. The book has since been republished in many forms and under a number of titles. Martin died on May 2, 1850, at the ripe old age of eighty-nine.

George Washington resigned his commission as commander in chief in 1784, "having now finished the work assigned me." He said good-bye to the ordinary soldiers of the Continental army in an emotional ceremony at Newburgh, New York, addressing them as "one patriotic band of brothers." And he bid a tearful farewell to his officers at Manhattan's Fraunces Tavern, which continues to serve food and drink today. Called back to

Washington
takes leave of his officers,
December 4, 1783.
*An 1883 illustration
by Howard Pyle.*

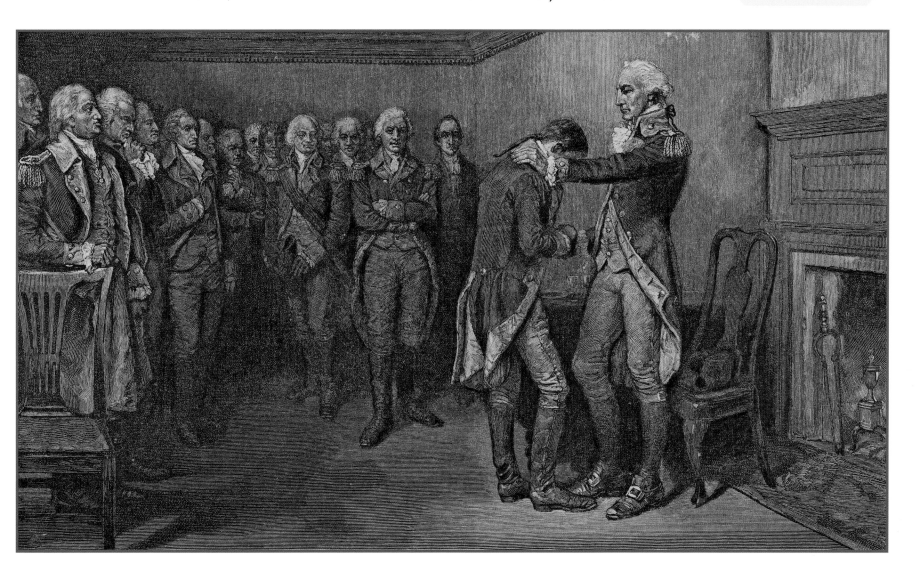

public service after a brief rest at his Mount Vernon plantation, Washington presided over the Constitutional Convention that drafted the United States Constitution in 1787, was elected president in 1789, and served two four-year terms. Afterward, he enjoyed less than three years of retirement at Mount Vernon. George Washington died of a throat infection on December 14, 1799, at the age of sixty-seven, after inspecting his lands on horseback in snow, hail, and freezing rain.

By the time Washington became president, the winter camp at Valley Forge had been reclaimed by farmers who owned the land. They had returned to their fields, planted crops, and torn down the army's log huts for firewood and fence posts. Few traces remained of the six-month winter ordeal that is recognized today as one of the defining moments of the Revolutionary War.

Some evidence suggests that Washington visited Valley Forge long after the war ended. According to one account, he showed up on horseback by himself one summer day, inspected what was left of the fortifications, and chatted with a local farmer, a Continental army veteran who had served as an enlisted man at the encampment during the winter of 1777 to 1778. As the two old-timers reminisced, Washington must have recalled the "patience and fortitude" he admired in his suffering troops, that so often in the past had brought him to the verge of tears. He knew that the decisive victory of the war was won not on any battlefield or at a diplomatic conference, but in the freezing huts and snowbound fields at Valley Forge. It was a victory of will—the will to endure and prevail over almost impossible odds.

Sergeant John Gibbs of New Hampshire spoke for his fellow enlisted men when he wrote: "It is verry [sic] remarkable that our Troops amidst all their Hardship which they Suffer Still keep a Steady Solid Fortitude of Mind."

What accounts for such uncommon patience and fortitude? Hessian Major Carl Baurmeister, who fought against the rebels, was convinced that the American army was kept from disintegrating because the rebels were inspired by "the spirit of liberty." British statesman Edmund Burke expressed the same belief, declaring that "a fierce spirit of liberty" was "stronger in the [American] colonies, probably, than in any other people of the earth."

At Valley Forge, Washington, who before the war had never commanded a military unit larger than a regiment, found within himself a rare capacity for leadership. He sustained the morale of an army on the point of collapse, fooled the British into believing that his forces were strong, and went on to defeat the colonial power's military might. And he met other challenges—overhauling the army's chaotic supply system, reckoning with a Congress that had little idea how to fight a war, and outwitting ambitious fellow officers who wanted to replace him.

Washington always insisted that credit for the American victory belonged to the men in the ranks who endured the winter at Valley Forge. Sharing hardships and sacrifices, they became comrades. It was the quiet heroism of those enlisted men, Washington said—"men oftentimes half starved, always in Rags, without pay and experiencing every species of distress which human nature is capable of undergoing"—that held the American army together during a critical time.

American enlisted men warm themselves at a campfire.

TIME LINE OF THE REVOLUTIONARY WAR

1765 On March 22 Parliament passes the Stamp Act, which taxes such items as legal documents, dice, and playing cards, causing widespread resentment among the American colonists.

1766 Stamp Act is repealed on March 18.

1767 On June 29, Parliament passes the Townshend Acts, which tax items including glass, paint, paper, and tea and incite the American colonists further.

1770 After being taunted by a group of colonists, British soldiers fire on a crowd in what became known as the Boston Massacre, March 5, killing five.

   In response to colonists' boycotts, Parliament cuts back on the Townshend Acts on April 12 but leaves the tax on tea.

1773 On December 16, in the Boston Tea Party, disguised Patriots sneak on board three ships and toss 342 casks of tea into Boston Harbor.

1774 Parliament passes the Coercive Acts to punish the colonists, closing Boston Harbor and forbidding town meetings.

   Twelve colonies send representatives to the First Continental Congress, beginning in Philadelphia on September 5.

1775 War breaks out on April 19, in the battles of Lexington and Concord.

   The Second Continental Congress begins on May 10.

   George Washington accepts position as commander of the Continental army, June 16.

1776   The Declaration of Independence is announced on July 4.

     The American rebels lose the Battle of Long Island on August 27, but Washington's daring escape with his troops on August 29 saves the Continental army.

     Washington defeats Hessian soldiers fighting for the British, after his dramatic crossing of the Delaware, December 25.

1777   The Marquis de Lafayette arrives in the United States on June 13 to fight for American independence.

     The Continental army is defeated at the Battle of Brandywine, September 11, and at the Battle of Germantown, October 4.

     General Gates and his troops defeat the British at the Battle of Saratoga.

     Washington and his soldiers camp at White Marsh.

     Washington leads his troops to their winter camp, Valley Forge, arriving December 19.

1778   General von Steuben arrives in Valley Forge on February 23.

     Official word of the alliance with France reaches Valley Forge, April 30.

     Washington's revived army leaves Valley Forge, June 19.

     The Continental army wins the Battle of Monmouth, June 28.

1780   The French army arrives in Newport, Rhode Island, to aid the American cause on July 10.

1781   The combined American and French forces win the Battle of Yorktown and the British surrender on October 19.

1783   The Treaty of Paris officially ends the Revolutionary War on September 3.

SOURCE NOTES

The following notes refer to the sources of quoted material. Each citation includes the first and last words or phrases of the quotation and the source. Unless otherwise noted, all references are to works cited in the Selected Bibliography.

Abbreviations used:

Bobrick—Benson Bobrick, *Angel in the Whirlwind*

Brady—Patricia Brady, *Martha Washington*

Brookhiser—Richard Brookhiser, *Founding Father*

Buchanan—John Buchanan, *The Road to Valley Forge*

Ellis—Joseph J. Ellis, *His Excellency*

Fleming—Thomas Fleming, *Washington's Secret War*

Flexner—James Thomas Flexner, *Washington*

Johnson—Paul Johnson, *George Washington*

Rebels—George F. Scheer and Hugh F. Rankin, *Rebels and Redcoats*

Scheer—George F. Scheer, ed., *Yankee Doodle Boy*

'76—Henry Steele Commager and Richard B. Morris, *The Spirit of 'Seventy-Six*

Unger—Harlow Giles Unger, *The Unexpected George Washington*

Page

INTRODUCTION: Against All Odds

xi   "starve, dissolve, or disperse": '76, p. 644

ONE: Bloody Footprints in the Snow

1   "walking . . . ground": Fleming, p. 12
"The army . . . blankets": Scheer, p. 74

2   "which kept . . . perform it with": Scheer, p. 74
"to call . . . soldier": Scheer, p. 18
"I [had] collected . . . my country": Scheer, p. 21
"this wooded . . . provisions": '76, p. 646

3   "a dreary . . . provided": Rebels, p. 304
"would share . . . inconvenience": Rebels, p. 304

4   "The idea . . . enemy": '76, p. 646
"not a morsel . . . eat": Scheer, p. 76
"We were now . . . need be": Scheer, p. 74

4   "perishing . . . finding any": Scheer,
     pp. 75–76
     "Fatigue . . . realities": Scheer, p. 76
     "They told me . . . call my own":
     Scheer, p. 76

5   "The General . . . anxious as now":
     Bobrick, p. 287

TWO: What Is to Become of the Army?

7–8   "a dangerous Mutiny . . . this
      Winter?": '76, p. 644

8   "straight as an Indian": Brookhiser,
      p. 107
      "He has so much . . . by his side":
      Brookhiser, p. 114

9   "He had . . . distance": Johnson, p. 7

10   "the best horseman . . . horseback":
      Brookhiser, p. 111
      "better than any other person in the
      Union": Brookhiser, p. 124
      "I beg . . . honored with": '76, p. 142

10–11 "so far . . . capacity": '76, p. 147

12   "The General . . . courage": Rebels,
      p. 153

13–14 "I made my escape . . . taken
      prisoner": Buchanan, pp. 59–60

14   "I think the game will be pretty well
      up": '76, p. 504
      "strike some Stroke": Ellis, p. 97
      "Come there . . . Hessians": Buchanan,
      p. 165
      "in a most . . . outwitted": Flexner, p. 98

17   "To expect . . . never will happen": Ellis,
      p. 77
      "give out . . . what it is": Bobrick, p. 238
      "the melancholy Truths": Ellis, p. 101
      "harass their troops to death":
      Buchanan, p. 200

19   "The foggy . . . us most": '76, p. 628

THREE: "We Were Determined to Persevere"

21   "to discharge the basic duties of the
      camp": Bobrick, p. 287
      "Why . . . discouraged": '76, p. 640

22   "that will be warm and dry": Rebels,
      p. 221
      "Our prospect . . . intolerable": Scheer,
      pp. 74–75
      "half . . . other time": Scheer, p. 76
      "No meat! No meat!": Fleming, p. 25

23   "The men . . . commanded": Fleming,
      p. 26
      "no less . . . naked": '76, p. 645

23   "destitute of every comfort": Fleming, p. 15

"Since . . . Genl.": '76, p. 645

"I do not . . . dissolve": Bobrick, p. 289

23–24 "I can assure . . . prevent": '76, pp. 645–646

24   "upon the ground . . . view": '76, p. 646

"temper . . . wrath": Brookhiser, p. 118

"We have . . . severe?": '76, p. 646

"We are still . . . weather": Rebels, p. 282

25   "Secret enemies . . . people": Buchanan, p. 297

"believe . . . enemy": Buchanan, p. 297

25–26 "My enemies . . . thought so by the enemy": Rebels, p. 299

FOUR: "A Cavalcade of Wild Beasts"

27   "Whole broadsides . . . British arms": Rebels, p. 320

28   "The bravery . . . kegs": Rebels, pp. 319–320

29   "Such feats . . . sir": '76, p. 637

"the quickest . . . manner": Fleming, p. 23

29–30 "For a week . . . campaign": '76, p. 649

31   "Three more . . . die fast": Fleming, p. 137

32   "of a lieutenant . . . bayonet": Scheer, p. 77

33   "brother soldiers": Fleming, p. 143

"Jethro . . . our regt": Fleming, p. 143

34   "a cavalcade of wild beasts": Ellis, p. 114

"The greatest . . . Camps": Buchanan, pp. 93–94

"this army . . . dissolve": '76, p. 644

35   "No pay! . . . No rum!": Bobrick, p. 291

36   "the skeleton . . . spirits": Fleming, p. 174

FIVE: "Congress Does Not Trust Me"

37   "The encampment . . . city": From an exhibit at Valley Forge

38   "tolerable good huts": From an exhibit at Valley Forge

39   "the cause": Unger, p. 119

"Pen-men": Ellis, p. 80

"military family": Unger, p. 119

40   "We are . . . teach": Bobrick, p. 295

"The Marquis . . . danger": Ellis, p. 115

"Treat him . . . son": Bobrick, p. 296

41   "that inestimable . . . cordiality": Bobrick, p. 296

"The situation . . . mutiny": '76, pp. 650–651

42   "The Country . . . heart": Buchanan, p. 288

"of every color and make": Fleming, p. 175

42   "a sort . . . bedcovers": Buchanan, p. 304

"the defects in our military system":
Fleming, p. 178

"Something . . . made": Fleming,
p. 176

"Congress . . . thus": Fleming, p. 175

42–44 "My dear General . . . long time ago":
Fleming, p. 175

44   "How could . . . cause?": Fleming,
p. 175

"Whenever . . . life": Ellis, p. 127

Six: The Secret Agent

45   "Several . . . madly": Bobrick, p. 118

"the general": Fleming, p. 184

"Mrs. Washington . . . each other":
Fleming, p. 185

46   "The General's . . . they were": Brady,
p. 121

47   "chatty . . . like": Buchanan, p. 8

"In the midst . . . song": Rebels, p. 310

"an excellent . . . same time": Rebels,
pp. 291–292

"a most powerful . . . shoulders":
Rebels, p. 310

49   "Torn clothes . . . together": Rebels,
p. 309

"My greatest . . . liberty": Rebels, p. 306

"The Baron . . . world": Fleming,
p. 210

50   "When I looked . . . aspect": Bobrick,
p. 303

"Our arms . . . Company": Buchanan,
p. 304

54   "The genius . . . does it": Rebels,
p. 307

55–56 "When some . . . properly performed":
Rebels, p. 308

56   "fits of passion . . . soldiers": Rebels,
p. 308

"My enterprise . . . expect": Rebels,
p. 308

"The Importance . . . obvious": Bobrick,
p. 336

Seven: A Great Day for General Washington

57   "such uncommon . . . fortitude":
Rebels, p. 314

"No body . . . History": Buchanan,
p. 285

58   "The alarm . . . quarters": Fleming,
p. 247

"I believe . . . joy": Rebels, p. 315

60   "did us . . . with us": Rebels, p. 314

"Be very sure . . . conjunction":
Bobrick, p. 339

60   "public celebration": Unger, p. 124

60–62   "the air . . . feelings": Rebels, p. 316

62   "swelling . . . Handel": Rebels, p. 316

        "Fifteen hundred . . . fortune": Unger, p. 124

        "loud huzzas . . . times": Rebels, pp. 316–317

62–63   "those dark . . . overwhelm us": Flexner, p. 118

63   "The possession . . . little": Ellis, p. 118

        "To us who had . . . accomplish this": Rebels, p. 317

EIGHT: Taking Back Philadelphia

65   "grow healthy . . . eat": Fleming, p. 277

66   "stout-looking . . . neat": Scheer, p. 83

        "We were . . . there": Scheer, pp. 83–84

        "The enemy . . . Barren Hill": Scheer, pp. 84–85

68   "finished or unfinished": Flexner, p. 119

NINE: "Band of Brothers"

70   "till the leaves . . . Heaven": Rebels, p. 331

71   "never saw the general . . . admirable": Fleming, p. 320

73   "While . . . occupation": Scheer, pp. 95–96

        "It was almost impossible to breathe": Scheer, p. 90

        "I singled . . . at the time": Scheer, p. 94

74   "We fight, get beat, rise and fight again": Fleming, p. 347

75   "Sir . . . liberty to step back": '76, p. 1233

76   "appeared to be much in liquor": Rebels, p. 494

77   "on this continent": Rebels, p. 494

        "May you . . . again!": Rebels, p. 495

        "In general . . . show": Rebels, p. 494

        "I noticed . . . about": Rebels, p. 495

79   "I would . . . with them": Fleming, p. 346

80   "Lafayette, we are here!": *The New Dictionary of Cultural Literacy*, Third Edition. Edited by E. D. Hirsch, Jr., Joseph F. Kett, and James Trefil. Copyright © 2002 by Houghton Mifflin Company. www.bartleby.com/59/11/lafayettemar.html

81   "having now finished the work assigned me": Ellis, p. 146

        "one patriotic band of brothers": Ellis, p. 146

82   "patience and fortitude": Rebels, p. 314

        "It is . . . Mind": Buchanan, p. 289

83   "the spirit of liberty": '76, p. 637

        "a fierce . . . earth": Buchanan, p. xiii

        "men . . . undergoing": Ellis, p. 111

SELECTED BIBLIOGRAPHY

Much has been written about the Valley Forge winter of 1777 to 1778, long recognized as a crucial turning point in the struggle for American independence. Contemporary scholarship has tended to debunk some of the myths that inevitably embellish momentous historic events. The hardships at Valley Forge, for instance, were due not as much to severe winter weather as to the incompetence of those officials responsible for the Continental army's supply system. And George Washington's eventual success depended as much on his savvy in dealing with political intrigues as on his merits as a military strategist.

I found two recent books invaluable in interpreting the events of that crucial winter: Thomas Fleming's *Washington's Secret War: The Hidden History of Valley Forge* (New York: HarperCollins, 2005) and John Buchanan's *The Road to Valley Forge: How Washington Built the Army That Won the Revolution* (Hoboken, NJ: John Wiley & Sons, 2004).

I am also indebted to two essential collections of writings and documents from the revolutionary era: Henry Steele Commager and Richard B. Morris's *The Spirit of 'Seventy-Six: The Story of the American Revolution as Told by Participants* (New York: Harper and Row, 1967) and George F. Scheer and Hugh F. Rankin's *Rebels and Redcoats: The American Revolution Through the Eyes of Those Who Fought and Lived It* (New York: World Publishing Company, 1957). George F. Scheer also edited Joseph Plumb Martin's autobiographical account of his wartime experiences, which has appeared in various formats and under different titles since its initial publication in 1830. My references are to the edition titled *Yankee Doodle Boy: A Young Soldier's Adventures in the American Revolution Told by Himself*, edited by George F. Scheer (New York: Holiday House, 1995).

George Washington is the best-documented figure of his time, yet he remains to many an enigmatic figure. Among recent biographies, Joseph J. Ellis's *His Excellency: George Washington* (New York: Alfred A. Knopf, 2004) is a particularly illuminating popular account by a Pulitzer Prize–winning historian. I also consulted James Thomas Flexner's *Washington: The Indispensable*

Man (Boston: Little, Brown, 1969, 1973, 1974), the single-volume edition of Flexner's monumental multi-volume biography. Paul Johnson's *George Washington: The Founding Father* (New York: HarperCollins, 2005) is a lively and incisive volume in the Eminent Lives series of brief biographies.

Among innumerable books on the Washington legend, I benefited especially from Richard Brookhiser's *Founding Father: Rediscovering George Washington* (New York: Free Press, 1997), Harlow Giles Unger's *The Unexpected George Washington: His Private Life* (Hoboken, NJ: John Wiley & Sons, 2006), and Marcus Cunliffe's *George Washington: Man and Monument* (Boston: Little, Brown, 1958).

Noteworthy biographical studies of other significant figures at Valley Forge include Patricia Brady's *Martha Washington: An American Life* (New York: Viking Penguin, 2005), Harlow Giles Unger's *Lafayette* (Hoboken, NJ: John Wiley & Sons, 2002), John McCauley Palmer's *General von Steuben* (Port Washington, NY: Kennikat Press, 1966, c. 1937), Ron Chernow's *Alexander Hamilton* (New York: Penguin Press, 2004), and Gregory D. Massey's *John Laurens and the American Revolution* (Columbia, SC: University of South Carolina Press, 2000).

Informative narrative histories of the Revo-lutionary War include Benson Bobrick's *Angel in the Whirlwind: The Triumph of the American Revolution* (New York: Simon & Schuster, 1997), Thomas Fleming's *Liberty! The American Revolution* (New York: Viking, 1997), Robert Middlekauff's *The Glorious Cause: The American Revolution 1763–1789* (New York: Oxford University Press, 1982), and Gordon S. Wood's *The American Revolution: A History* (New York: Modern Library, 2002).

Today, the site of the 1777–1778 Continental army encampment belongs to the American people. The Valley Forge National Historical Park, an expansive parkland, is enjoyed by strollers, dog walkers, and history buffs, and features monuments, a memorial chapel, and both historical and re-created structures. Scattered about the park are replicas of the log huts that sheltered the suffering troops more than two hundred years ago. The stone house that Washington used as his headquarters is still standing and is furnished much as it was in 1778: Visitors can peek into the bedroom where George and Martha slept and the office where Washington worked. A welcome center offers a short film, a well-stocked bookshop, and museum exhibits depicting the quiet valor of those "dear ragged Continentals," who prevailed against all odds. The park grounds are open from 6 A.M. to 10 P.M. year-round, the welcome center from 9 A.M. to 5 P.M. daily.

To visit online, see www.nps.gov/vafo.

The Valley Forge National Historical Park Archives and Library, with their many specialized books and collections of diaries, letters, and other writings from Valley Forge, are open to the general public by appointment only: phone 610-296-2593, fax 610-783-1060.

PICTURE CREDITS

The American Revolution: A Picture Sourcebook by John Grafton (New York: Dover Publications, 1975): pages 3, 19, 24, 25, 32, 33, 34, 37, 40, 49, 51, 55, 64 (bottom), 66, 74, 75, 83

The Colonial Williamsburg Foundation. Gift of Mr. John D. Rockefeller, Jr.: page 6

Mary Evans Picture Library: pages 48 (left), 48 (right), 52

Russell Freedman: pages 29, 30 (top left), 38 (top left)

Library of Congress: pages ii, 9, 11, 15, 16, 26, 30 (bottom), 31, 35, 38 (bottom), 39 (right), 46, 53, 54, 59, 64 (top), 67, 69, 71, 72, 78, 79

Picture Collection, The Branch Libraries, The New York Public Library, Astor, Lenox and Tilden Foundations: pages xi, xii, 5, 13, 18, 20, 22, 28, 43, 44, 58, 61, 63, 76, 81

Wikipedia (public domain): pages 39 (left), 45, 57, 80

INDEX

Page numbers in *italics* refer to illustrations.

A

Adams, John, 10

African Americans, as Continental army soldiers, 32–33

American Indians, as Continental army soldiers, 33, 42, 47–48, 66

American Revolution. *See* Revolutionary War

American Turtle (submarine), 27

American War of Independence. *See* Revolutionary War

Angell, Israel, 31

Antoinette, Marie (queen of France), *58*

B

Baltimore, Md., as site of Continental Congress, 14

Barren Hill (Pa.) camp, 66

Base (early form of baseball), 48

"Battle of the Kegs, The," *28,* 28–29

Battles of the Mid-Atlantic States, map of, *ix*

Baurmeister, Carl, 82–83

bayonets, *52,* 52–53, *53.*
    See also hand-to-hand combat

Blue Book, The (See *Regulations for Order and Discipline of the Troops of the United States*)

Boston, Mass.
    British occupation of, 8

siege of, 12

boxing matches, *48,* 48

Brandywine Creek, Pa., battle of, 7, 18, 39, 40, *67*

British army
    in Boston, 12
    in New York, 12–14
    in Philadelphia, 3, 7, 18, 19, 23
    surrender of, 75–76, *76,* 76–77
    See also Continental army; Revolutionary War; *names of specific battles*

Brooks, John, 30

"Brown Bess" (musket), 52, *52*

Burgoyne, John, 19

Burke, Edmund, 83

Burr, Aaron, 79

Bushnell, David, 27–28

C

Cambridge, Mass., as site of Washington's headquarters, 12

camp fever, 30

camp followers, in Valley Forge encampment, 33–34, *34*

Clewly, Lucy, 80

Clinton, Henry, 64, *64,* 65, 68

clothing, worn in Valley Forge encampment, 23, *25, 33,* 65.
    See also uniforms, worn by Continental army

Cobb, David, 75

Index

100